The FLIGHT *of* DRAGONS

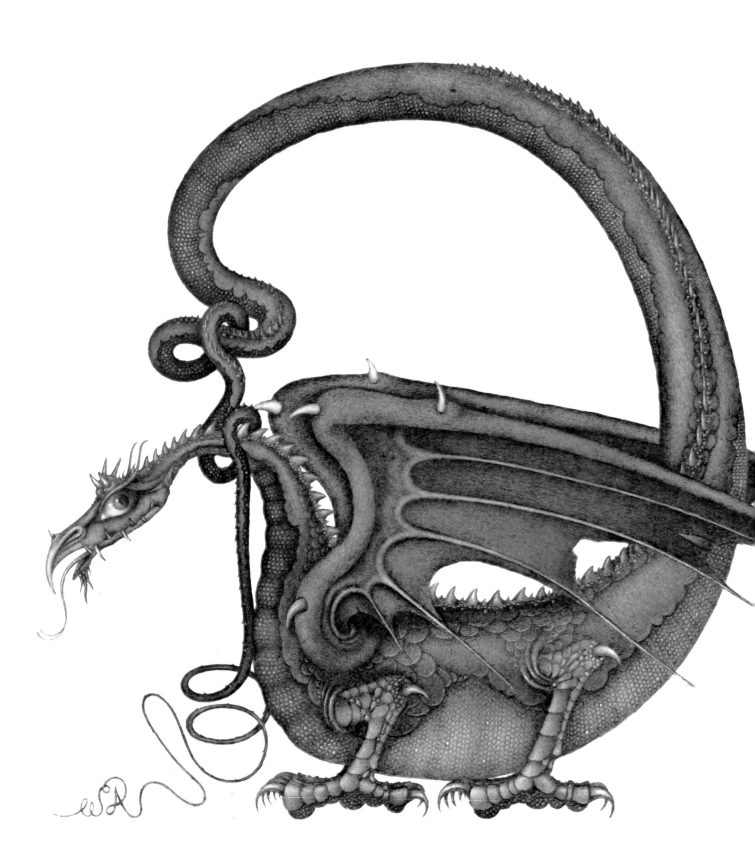

The FLIGHT of DRAGONS

PETER DICKINSON
ILLUSTRATED BY WAYNE ANDERSON

Paper Tiger

Paper Tiger
An imprint of Collins & Brown Ltd
London House
Great Eastern Wharf
Parkgate Road
London
SW11 4NQ

This edition first published in Great Britain in 1998
by Collins & Brown Ltd

Previously published by Pierrot Publishing Ltd and
The New English Library 1979

10 9 8 7 6 5 4 3 2 1

British Library Cataloguing-in-Publication Data:
A catalogue record for this book is available from
the British Library

ISBN 1 85028 411 3

Printed in Spain by Artes Gráficas Toledo, S.A.
D.L.TO: 154-1998

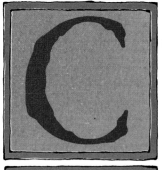

CONTENTS

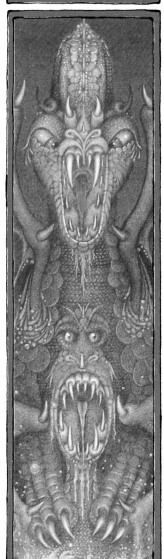

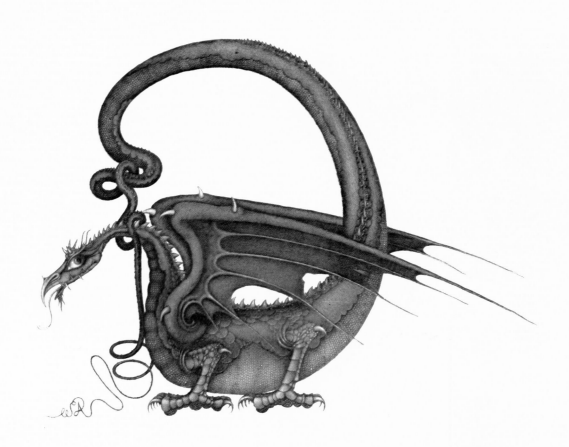

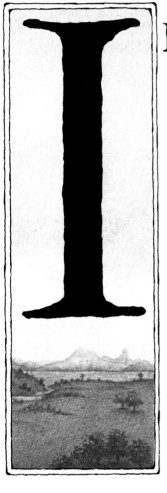

I NTRODUCTION

This book is about winged, fire-breathing dragons. There are three possible
views about these glorious animals:
(i)   They are completely legendary.
(ii)   They are largely legendary, but contain elements based on second-hand
accounts of real animals — crocodiles, boa constrictors, sting rays and so on.
(iii) They really existed.
I take the third view.

I am not going to *prove* that ninety-foot lizards once floated in the skies of earth
and scorched whole villages with plumes of flame, because I don't think it can be
proved. For reasons which I shall discuss I think it impossible that the fossil
remains of a true dragon can ever be found; and for other reasons it is very
unlikely that cave-paintings will ever come to light, showing the tribal heroes of
the Stone Age battling with this ferocious enemy.

But I can put together a coherent theory which is at least as probable as the
theory that dragons are completely legendary.

It is the coherence that matters. It is no use my showing that there is a possible mechanism by which dragons could have breathed fire, and another by which they could have flown, and yet another to account for the supposed magical nature of dragon's blood, and my then saying that these could possibly all have been attributes of the same animal — that is not how animals evolve. However strange the life-form a species may adopt, it all centres round a particular specialisation. Once the creature has, so to speak, decided to get its living in one particular way, everything about it must be an inevitable aspect of that one process. So if dragons existed, it had to be the same with them.

This book is called *The Flight of Dragons* because my theory is that the particular specialisation of dragons was that they evolved a unique mode of flight. They grew to their enormous size because size was necessary if they were to fly successfully. They breathed fire because they had to. Their "blood" had seemingly magical properties because a particular chemical reaction was necessary for their mode of flight. And so on. At the remoter fringes of the theory I think I can show how the life-form that evolved through this specialisation came to prefer for its diet young ladies of noble breeding.

The reader may be surprised to find that most of my evidence is taken from fictional accounts of dragons — not merely ancient legend which might be supposed to have some connection with still more ancient fact, but modern fiction as well — accounts which both the writer and reader of such books usually suppose to be pure invention. I will discuss the validity of such evidence later. For the moment I must ask you to try not to think of my use of these passages as pure whimsy.

FLIGHT

"The dragon hovered above them. Ninety feet was he, maybe, from tip to tip of his vast membranous wings, that shone in the new sunlight like gold-shot smoke, and the length of his body was no less, but lean, arched like a greyhound, clawed like a lizard, and snake-scaled."

Ursula Le Guin *The Farthest Shore*

The problem can be put very simply. How did a creature of the size recorded stay aloft, and indeed hover?

There are a few pure gliders in nature, such as flying fish and flying squirrels, which can only stay aloft for very limited periods. Apart from these there are three types of flying animal — birds, bats and insects. The fossil record contains a fourth type, now extinct — pterodactyls.

The flight of all of these depends on two linked laws:

(i)   The air-pressure below the wing must be greater than the air-pressure above the wing. This difference gives the animal its "lift".

(ii)   The lift must be greater than the total weight of the animal.

The question of weight is crucial, so the next step is to attempt to estimate the weight of a dragon. Only the roughest calculations are possible, but they will do. The dragon described by Ursula Le Guin was ninety feet long, but how lean is "lean"? In a later passage in the same book there is an account of two men climbing onto a dragon's back by four steps, which means five risers. Both men were tired, or in the last stages of exhaustion — eighteen inches would be as much as they could manage at a step, which gives a thickness through the body

---

AD 793: Here dire forewarnings were come over the land of the Northumbrians and sadly terrified the people. There were tremendous lightnings, and fiery dragons were seen flying in the air.

The Anglo-Saxon Chronicle

of about seven and a half feet. We will reduce it further, to six feet — really absurdly slim for a ninety-foot beast, and we will assume it tapers evenly from this thickest point — unlikely, but I am making all these assumptions to achieve the minimum reasonable weight. This gives us a body-volume of roughly eight hundred cubic feet. All flying animals evolve weight-saving strategies, such as hollow bones, but there is a limit to what these can achieve; ignoring the weight of the wings, a body of this volume would weigh about 20,000 pounds.

The record in the animal kingdom for lift is held by the Canada goose, which lifts 4.2 pounds of body-weight for every square foot of wing. The swallow, by comparison, lifts 0.3 lb. Apart from birds, the record belongs to the bumble-bee, which lifts 2.5 lb. The difference is accounted for by the peculiarity of feathers, which allow air to pass through them from above to below but not in the opposite direction, and so increase the pressure difference. Some artists have drawn dragons with feathered wings, but they always look wrong; so it is fair to allow our dragon a lifting ability equivalent to the bumble-bee; then to lift 40,000 lb., it would need around 16,000 square feet of wing. Give it a normal sort of wing shape — say one third of the body-length from leading to trailing edge, roughly rectangular and tapering a little at the tips — and it must have a wing-span of over 600 feet. This is not merely six times the span of the dragon Orm Embar, described by Miss Le Guin in the quotation at the head of this section, it is also aerodynamically quite impossible.

It may be argued that the descriptions from which I have deduced these figures are inaccurate, but even if we halve all the dimensions given we are still left with an animal which either couldn't fly or would be grossly unmanoeuvrable. And bear in mind that in making my estimates I have loaded all guesses as far as possible in the dragon's favour. For instance, both the Canada goose and the bumble-bee, which carry their weight so efficiently, have dumpy bodies. Their main mass consists of the flight-muscles, located as close as possible to the wing-roots. Fliers with differently structured bodies need much bigger wing areas, more comparable with the swallow at 0.3 lb. per square foot, or even the butterfly at 0.025.

We can approach the whole problem from a different angle. The largest flying birds — the Kori bustard, the white pelican, the mute swan, the California condor — all have a weight of around 27 lb. The largest wing-spans are about 13 feet. In the fossil record there were the pterosaur *Pteranodon* and the super-condor *Teratornis* which are thought to have weighed 40 lb. and 45 lb. respectively. But both of these almost certainly were unable to do more than soar in rising currents

---

Once more . . . he had underestimated dragon capabilities. The ground was not rushing up to meet him. To the contrary, it was far, far below him, odd little patches of wood alternating with open country. He was at least a couple of thousand feet up and climbing rapidly . . . . Evidently a dragon's great muscular power could lift him rapidly to soaring heights. But from then on it must be a matter of his riding the available winds and thermals.

Gordon R. Dickson The Dragon and the George

of air. Curiously, the record weight for a flying animal is now held by man. The 1976 experiments in man-powered flight have shown that it is possible to lift a man's body-weight and that of his machine — around 400 lb. — over a mile-long course by the use of enormous wings. The price has been almost total unmanoeuverability and a maximum speed of a few m.p.h. There is in fact a natural limit on the weight and size of any successful flying animal. (The flying man would not have made a successful species: his wings were incredibly fragile, he was utterly exhausted at the end of each flight, and he crashed at least twenty times before once finishing the course.) So anything as big as a dragon could not possibly have flown.

And yet they did. They were no mere soarers, either, relying on cliffs like the *Pteranodon*, or wave effects like the albatross. They flew efficiently and quickly. The dragon Smaug made the flight from the Lonely Mountain to Laketown (a journey which had taken Bilbo and the dwarves three days in the opposite direction) within the first half of one night — and there are no thermals to provide free lift at night, either. The dragon Kalessin took Ged and Arren from Selidor to Ravnor — half the width of Earthsea — in a few days. But even more noteworthy than speed is the ability to hover. Without the help of thermals only small birds and insects can hover for any length of time. A bird the size of a pigeon can manage it for a few seconds. Anything larger than that cannot achieve the rapid wing-beat required.

Clearly there is something badly wrong with our assumptions, something that cannot simply be put down to an error in the original description. Reduce

the length of a dragon to, say, twenty feet and give it a forty-foot wing-span and it still cannot be made to fly. Increase the efficiency of the wing beyond anything else known in the natural kingdom and the same is true. What does that leave?

It leaves weight.

In order to fly, dragons must have been almost weightless.

If progressively larger birds are now considered, the power-required curve shifts upward and to the right, while the power available also increases, but not so much as the power required. Very large birds, such as the larger African vulture, have apparently only just sufficient power to fly horizontally, and cannot hover even very briefly . . . It cannot fly at any speed slower than some minimum . . . and it must therefore accelerate to this speed by running along the ground before it can become airborne . . .

Colin J. Pennycuick Animal Flight

The cheering stopped and the joy was turned to dread. So it was that the dragon did not find them quite unprepared.

Before long, so great was his speed, they could see him as a spark of fire rushing towards them and growing ever huger and more bright . . . Every warrior was armed, every arrow and dart was ready, and the bridge to the land was thrown down and destroyed, before the roar of Smaug's terrible approach grew loud, and the lake rippled red as fire beneath the awful beating of his wings.

J. R. R. Tolkien The Hobbit

Nature into Image: Suppose all flying animals became extinct, and all accurate portrayals of them perished, but artists continued to draw them from memory and description, and then from tradition. The process by which an image evolved would be gradual. The bee *(left)* represents an early stage; the wing is simplified, the body exaggerated, so that already it is doubtful whether the creature could fly. The bird *(below)* is close to the final image that might evolve. Note the emphasis on beak, eye and talons, and how the aerodynamics have become implausible – one feather providing the leading edge of the wings, and others concealing a number of anatomical problems.

The Flying Brick

This imaginary creature has wings made of dinner plates, one on each side. It cannot fly particularly well because two nine-inch dinner plates are only just enough to lift one brick. It looks like this:

Some authorities refer to the Big Brick, whose body is twice as large in each direction, and so consists of eight bricks, needing sixteen dinner plates to lift them. It must therefore look like this:

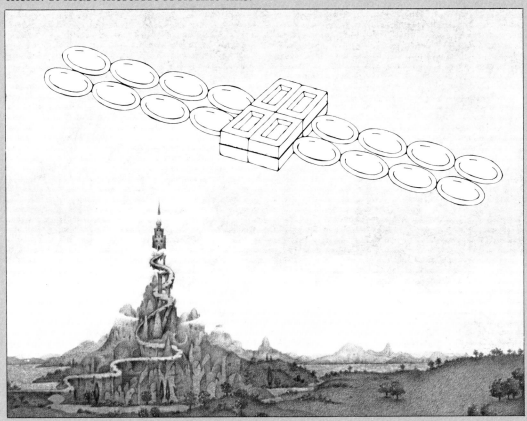

The Big Brick may be a conceivable creature, but the Tyrannosaurus Brick is not. It is supposed to have a body six times as big in each direction as the common Flying Brick. That is to say its body consists of 216 bricks — not a very large pile, four feet long, two feet wide and one and a half feet high. But to lift it 432 plates would be needed, arranged in wings six plates deep and thirty-six plates wide — a wing span well over fifty feet.

FIERY BREATH

"These dragons grow exceeding big, and from their mouths cast forth a most pestilential breath, like unto thick smoke rising from a fire. At their destined time they gather together, and developing wings they begin to raise themselves into the air. Then, by God's good judgment, being too heavy they fall into a certain river which springs from Paradise, and therein they perish wholly. All those who dwell round about attend the season of the dragons, and when they see that one has fallen they wait yet seventy days. Then they go down and discover the bare bones of the dragon, that they may take the carbuncle that is rooted in the forehead thereof."

Jordanus *The Wonders of the East*

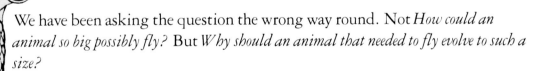

We have been asking the question the wrong way round. Not *How could an animal so big possibly fly?* But *Why should an animal that needed to fly evolve to such a size?*

When I first came across the confused but extremely interesting passage from

It was dreadfully hot, even high up in the air where the Prince hung invisible . . . the steam and smoke, and the flames which the Firedrake spouted like foam from his nostrils, would have daunted even the bravest man. The sides of the hill, too, were covered with the blackened ashes of his victims, whom he had roasted when they came out to kill him.

Andrew Lang Prince Prigio

Jordanus quoted above, I was chiefly concerned with the idea that it was a description of a mating-flight. I still think this may well be true, but I will come back to that aspect of it later (and also to the extremely rapid decay of the dragon's body, and the association with jewels.) But for the moment I want to concentrate on the curious business of variable weight.

Jordanus, of course, had never seen a dragon. I think it improbable that any had survived to within a thousand years of his time. Like many another learned man he was copying his story from some other manuscript, perhaps combining two or three sources and trying to make sense of them where they contradicted each other. These sources would also be copies of yet other copies and re-tellings, going back to a time when the tradition lived only in the spoken word, and eventually to some traveller who had actually seen the dragon-flight. Still dragon-lore dies hard, though it may become twisted in the telling. In particular the punctuation of early manuscripts is non-existent, so that it is difficult to tell which bits of the argument really belong together.

As I say, my first idea when I read this passage was that it described a mating-flight. The phrase "developing wings" supported this notion. I thought perhaps that dragons flew only for the mating-flight (like some of the social insects) and that after the flight the successful males died. I was still of this mind when one day I happened to see on television an old news-reel film of the wreck of the airship Hindenburg, and almost in a flash all my ideas changed. As I watched the monstrous shape crumpling and tumbling in fiery fragments, with the smoke-clouds swirling above, I said to myself *It flamed and it fell*, and my mind made the leap to Jordanus. All the pieces I had been considering shook themselves into a different shape. I saw that the Hindenburg was not merely a

---

Here it comes, ladies and gentlemen, and what a sight it is, a thrilling one, a marvellous sight . . . The sun is striking the windows of the observation deck on the westward side and sparkling like glittering jewels on the background of black velvet . . . Oh! Oh! Oh! . . . It's burst into flames . . . get out of the way, please, oh my, this is terrible, oh my, get out of the way, please, it is burning, bursting into flames and is falling . . . Oh! This is one of the worst . . . Oh! It's a terrific sight . . . Oh! and all the humanity . . ."

Radio commentator: *Wreck of the Hindenburg*

. . . Icarus, intoxicated by excitement and heedless of his father's warning, soared upward towards the sun. His impious presumption was punished by Phoebus Apollo, whose angry heat melted the wax so that the wings fell off and Icarus plummeted headlong to his death.

That is the myth . . . It is surely possible, however, that it was a hot-air balloon which Daedalus constructed; a huge bag of thin, treated animal skin, heated by a fire of wood or dry grass and bearing a carriage in which a man might ride. . . . a careless error misdirected the flames, causing the frail craft to flare into sudden incadescence and dive earthward in a strange ball of fire.

Patrick Abbott *Airship*

very big machine which flew — it was a machine which could fly only because it was very big. Other answers slotted into place.

(i)   Dragons could fly because most of their bodies were hollow, and filled with a lighter-than-air gas.

(ii)   Dragons needed an enormous body to hold enough gas to provide lift for the total weight of the beast.

(iii)   Dragons did not need enormous wings, because they used them only for propulsion and manoeuvering.

(iv)   Dragons breathed fire because they had to. It was a necessary part of their specialised mode of flight.

Jordanus says that the dragons begin to raise themselves into the air and then "being too heavy" they fall. It is at once clear that he is describing something he doesn't understand. No animal which has gone to the lengths of evolving flight can also be too heavy to fly. But suppose what the original traveller saw was indeed a mating-flight, then we can make sense of the scene by linking this sentence with the one in front of it, about the dragons breathing out their fiery and pestilential breath.

The flight would not have been like that of the males of a social insect competing in pursuit of their new-hatched queen; it must have been something more comparable to the behaviour of rutting deer, in which the males battle with each other for the right to fertilise the females; but where stags fight with their antlers the dragons fought with their flaming breath. As with most mating contests this would have been a highly ritualised form of battle, with little damage inflicted and most of the warfare consisting of pure display — vast plumes of noxious smoke, great blasts of flame — as impressive in its way as the

. . . keep watch in thine own person, and then thou shalt see the dragons fighting in the shape of monster animals. But at last they shall go in dragon-shape aloft in the air; and last of all, when they shall have grown weary of their dire and frightful combat, they will fall in the shape of two little pigs . . .

The Mabinogion *trans: Gwyn Jones and Thomas Jones*

(overleaf) Encounter between two young dragons, mature enough for flight but not yet ready to take a full part in the mating-dance (page 68). Such meetings would have been dangerous, not because the combatants might damage each other, but because they might be stimulated to breathe excessive amounts of flame before their gas-production system was adequate to replace the loss. But at such meetings as these the skills necessary to survive in the mating-dance would have been gradually mastered. (Note that here and throughout this book the artist has adhered closer to the conventional portrayal of dragons in matters of wing-shape and body-structure than to what I believe to have been the truth. For details see pages 34 and 42.)

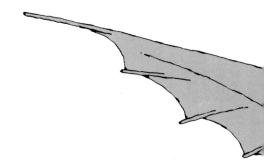

tail-feathers of the peacock or the song of the nightingale. There was, however, a danger. Should a dragon in an excess of sexual fervour flame off too much of its gas it would lose buoyancy and plummet to earth, and die.

The curious detail about the dragons "developing wings" now makes sense. Dragon-wings were comparatively small (though still far larger than the wings of any other flying creature). As they were not needed to support the weight of the dragon they could also be comparatively fragile, and so would be carried folded close along the body for protection until they were needed. The original observer of the mating ritual would be likely to be so impressed by the sheer size of the dragons' bodies that he might not even notice the wings until they were suddenly spread for flight. (Anybody who has watched a small beetle produce, as if from nowhere, its filmy wings and float away on the wind can perhaps imagine the effect.)

There is one more link I must provide. Why did the dragons burn their excess gas, instead of simply belching it out? The answer lies in another well-known custom of dragons. They laired in caves, and stayed there for long periods. I imagine they must have had some control over their gas-production and were able to manufacture more or less, according to need; but there would have to be both upper and lower limits to this control — a major metabolic process cannot be completely shut down. So even when they were at rest in their caves there

---

The Dragon lived in a black and silent valley which had once been green with pasture. His den looked like a railway tunnel without any signals or track. Those who had seen him, by moonlight, knew that he was bigger than four carthorses, and sleek, and black, and shiny. Like all black dragons he seldom came out except at night, because his eyes were weak. And in the day, these eyes were all that could be seen of him.

Robert Bolt The Thwarting of Baron Bolligrew

He had no more than rolled over before Rusk put his hoof upon his chest. He sprang up angrily only to see in the pale white light of the moon a huge serpent, three hundred palms in length, twisting towards him on its belly. Its eyes glared like two round emeralds, and from its nostrils bright streams of fire belched forth. He grasped his scimitar and struck the reptile a heavy blow, but it only hissed more loudly and breathed its venomous fire upon him until he was scorched by the heat.

Firdusi The Shahnameh

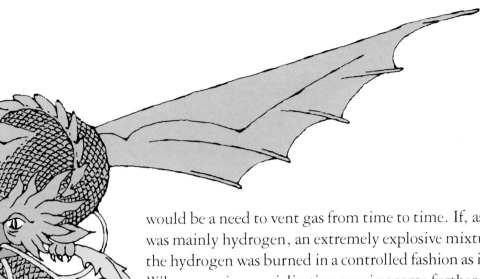

would be a need to vent gas from time to time. If, as I propose to show, the gas was mainly hydrogen, an extremely explosive mixture would be formed unless the hydrogen was burned in a controlled fashion as it left the dragon's body. Where a major specialisation requires some further adaptation to make it effective, that adaptation usually evolves. If dragons needed to burn their breath in order to survive, nature would provide a means.

What means? One is tempted by the idea of an electric spark, but the existing animals, such as the electric eel, which are able to produce the necessary voltage for a spark are specialists in electricity. I am extremely reluctant to propose any adaptation that does not arise from the original specialisation, so I think it more likely that the ignition system was chemical. In order to produce the hydrogen the dragon's body was already a series of chemical retorts, so some mixture leading to spontaneous combustion on contact with air is much more plausible. Vaguely similar devices do exist in nature. For instance the bombadier beetles of the *Brachinus* family have a defensive weapon which consists of spitting out droplets of liquid at a temperature of several hundred degrees; the chemicals to achieve the effect are produced by two separate glands and do not combine until they are clear of the beetle's mouth.

Whatever the mechanism, dragons learnt to breathe flame because they had to. For reasons I will describe later, the habit of lairing in safe caves was essential to their survival, and unless the explosive gases they produced were burned off, those caves would cease to be habitable. The use of the flaming breath as a weapon, and as a form of sexual display, evolved from something which already existed as part of the mechanism of flight. To the Stone Age hero, confronting those pulses of fury at the cave mouth, fire must have seemed the primary aspect of the dragon, but like everything else in nature, however strange, it had evolved along a logical path.

Mnementh . . . craned his sinuous neck round in a wide sweep . . . Then, without warning to his rider, he folded his wings and dove toward an especially thick patch, braking his descent with neck-snapping speed. As Mnementh belched fire, F'lar watched with intense satisfaction as the Thread curled into black dust and floated harmlessly to the forests below.

Anne McCaffrey Dragonquest

Legs and Wings

When a professional artist draws a dragon he gives it a wing like a bat's, or sometimes a bird's.

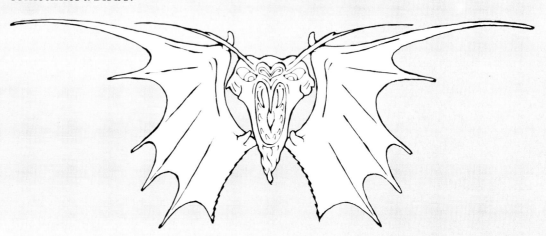

He is aware that all flying animals have evolved their wings by an adaptation of the fore-limbs, on these lines:

Then he has a problem about the legs. If the front limbs have become wings then the animal can only have two, but that always looks wrong: everybody knows dragons had four legs. But if he gives it four he has a six-limbed vertebrate — impossible. It is interesting that the problem doesn't exist with drawings of angels and devils, and even pegasi, because the artist is aware that he is drawing something which is either quite imaginary or else a representation of a non-material being. He can clap on a pair of wings at the shoulder-blades and not bother about limb-count or musculature. But dragons are different.

Ask a child, with no anatomical preconceptions, to draw a dragon and he will produce a wing-structure something like this:

This is more like a fin than a wing, and has ribs like an umbrella. Evolutionarily it would be a modification of the spine or of the rib-cage. The Pelycosaurs had a single spinal "sail", and the extant gliding lizard *Draco volans* (note the name) has "wings" based on a fold of skin and supported on elongated ribs which fold against the body when not in use.

A structure like this would not be very strong, but it would not need to be. On the other hand it would be very light, and would also need comparatively little weight of muscle to operate it.

DRAGON BLOOD

"In the legendary Hsia dynasty (c. 2205 to 1557 BC) . . . one of the kings collected foam from the mouths of two ancestors who appeared in his palace in the form of dragons. He put the foam in a box. No one in succeeding generations dared open the box. At the end of the reign of the tenth king of the Chou dynasty (c. 110 to 221 BC) the box was opened. The foam spread through the palace. The king made his wives appear naked before it. It became a black lizard and entered the women's apartments. An extraordinary pregnancy occurred."

Larousse Encyclopedia of Mythology

Here, even more than with the extract from Jordanus, we are in the realm of almost-legend— fact and fantasy so intwined as to make something which is not quite either. The story is normally explained as an attempt by the Chou kings to renew the legitimacy and power of their rule by claiming to incorporate into their blood-line the dragon-ancestors of the Hsia. Or the details about the lizard and the pregnancy could be interpreted as a pure anxiety-fantasy, typical of societies in which the ruler's honour involved his having a large number of wives whom only he could approach. But even fantasy has to be fuelled with a small amount of fact, and often it is the bizarre detail which shows where this fact is buried. Under what conceivable circumstances does a monarch, whose palace is rapidly filling with a dangerous chemical, order his wives to appear naked before it?

For instance, take dragon's blood. You know that it is banned . . . An ordinary necromancer like myself can only get it at great risk and expense, and our exotic suppliers have to endanger themselves to get it for us.

Diana Wynne Jones Charmed Life

Suppose cause and effect really operated in the other direction. These noxious clouds have been released and are fuming through the building, and their touch is corrosive enough to rot delicate fabrics. Not all the people escape. Some are overcome and when at last the fumes clear their bodies are found, naked and charred. An ancient story-teller, the Chinese equivalent of Jordanus, hears the tale after many repetitions and tries to make sense of it in his own terms. The substance was known to emanate from dragons, and just as European monarchs have tended to take the most powerful beast they know of, the lion, as their symbol, so Chinese emperors laid claim to dragons. The substance frothed when the box was opened and lips froth, so it must have come from the lips of two very powerful dragons, the imperial ancestors. (Or could it conceivably be one of the chemicals which ignited the dragon's breath, in which case it could really have come from the lips, and might well react violently with air when the box was opened?) The king in his wisdom knew how to placate these ancestors . . . and so on.

I have chosen this episode because it is both strange and familiar. The strangeness because of the cultural background differing from ours, and the familiarity from the recognition of the terrifying properties of substances emanating from the dragon's metabolism. In European legend we tend to describe all these substances as "blood". When Hercules slew the Hydra he dipped his arrows in its blood to make them poisonous. One of his victims was the centaur Nessus who, dying, told Deianira to soak a shirt in his blood. Eventually Hercules put that shirt on, and the poison of the Hydra was still so strong in it that he too died, howling.

I could list a hundred such episodes, all pointing to the same thing — the "blood" of dragons was magical, or poisonous, or corrosive, or all three. The many accounts which refer to the inner fires of the dragon are probably also misunderstandings of this same phenomenon. I do not believe in a creature which carries around a mass of material at several hundred degrees, but I can believe quite easily in one whose metabolism involved quantities of "burning" fluid, that is to say quite powerful acids. To believe this all I have to do is to answer the question *Why?* That is to say *What evolutionary advantage was it to the dragon to be filled with a liquid of such a nature?* The answer will only make sense if it is shown to be essential to the main specialisation of flight.

We have seen that the flight of dragons must have depended on their ability to

---

There was a man of that Town whose name was Winckelriedt, who was banished for man-slaughter: this man promised, if he might have his pardon, and be restored again to his former Inheritance, that he would combate with that dragon, and by God's help destroy him: which thing was granted unto him with great joyfulness. Wherefore he was recalled home, and in the presence of many people went forth to fight with the Dragon, whom he slew and overcame, whereat for joy he lifted up his sword imbrued in the Dragon's bloud, in token of victory, but the bloud distilled down from his sword upon his body, and caused him instantly to fall down dead.

Edward Topsell The History of Serpents

make their bodies weightless, or almost weightless, in air. To do this they needed to fill large cavities — cavities which in fact composed the major part of their body-structure — with a lighter-than-air gas. (The possibility of their producing near-vacuums in these cavities is not worth considering — it would demand huge strength, and therefore weight, to withstand the air-pressure.) Helium is light enough to do the job, but is a most unlikely candidate, an inert gas, present in minute quantities in the atmosphere, but not known to play much part in the metabolism of any animal. Hydrogen is far more plausible — a very light abundant gas, violently inflammable when mixed with oxygen, and present in an accessible form in a substance already common in the digestive systems of all vertebrates — hydrochloric acid.

Natural species do not evolve out of nothing, however mysterious or absurd the forms they eventually achieve. The throat of the baleen whale, the drilling head of the teredo worm, the flotation chamber of the nautilus — all these evolved from something already present in the ancestral animal, some so-far-neglected feature which nature gradually exaggerated into the weird mechanism it has now become. So with dragons. In attempting to reconstruct their form and life-pattern I must not invent anything, however convenient. I must look for existing inventions which nature could improve and recombine, such as the hydrochloric acid we all must brew inside ourselves in order to stay alive.

We also carry around quite large quantities of the other essential element in the reaction needed to produce hydrogen. That is to say, the bones of vertebrates are largely composed of calcium. The reaction at its simplest looks like this:

$$Ca_{(s)} + 2HCl_{(aq)} \rightarrow H_2 + CaCl_{2(aq)}$$

That is to say hydrochloric acid reacts with calcium to produce hydrogen with calcium chloride in aqueous solution as a by-product.

Of course biological chemistry is never as simple as that. There would have to be all sorts of other substances to control and modify the reactions, as well as those needed to ignite the gas when it was vented. The innards of the dragon were a complex chemical factory, with not only hydrogen as the end-product but all sorts of other substances which had either to be used or excreted. Evidently it was one of these substances which was somehow closed into the Hsia box. Others account for the "pestilential" nature of dragon breath, even when not ignited,

---

These Indian serpents fly at night and let fall drops of their urine or sweat, which occasions the skins of persons who are not on their guard to putrefy.

Strabo The Geography

He grasped his sword with both hands and struck with all his might from underneath. The sword plunged in up to the hilt. The dragon writhed in terrible death-throes, spewing forth both blood and poison, so that it was a wondrous sight. Jatmundr protected himself with his shield until it fell apart, but by that time the dragon was dead. The Jatmundr Saga Ljufa

and yet others for the notorious trail of slime which dragons left behind them, and which defiled the countryside anywhere near a dragon's lair, and which I believe helps to account for the well-known dragon habit of gold-nesting, i.e. sleeping on treasure-hoards. (see page 94.)

Despite these chemical complexities the main body-structure of the dragon consisted of a series of cavities, or vats, mostly filled with hydrogen but secreting down the walls and gathering at the bottom the powerful acid needed to keep the reaction going. Should one of these chambers be pierced from below — and remember that they composed most of the dragon's body, so that a stroke from below would have every chance of piercing one — two things would happen. First, the acid would flow out and react with anything it touched — the blade that had made the wound, the arm that held the blade, even the dragon's own flesh. Second, the cavity itself would become useless, and this in turn would have two results: the dragon would no longer be able to fly, and it would no longer have excess gas to breathe out as flame.

I shall return later to the essential vulnerability of dragons to cutting weapons. For the moment I must emphasise a different consequence of the violent chemistry of the dragon's metabolism. Flight was achieved by a controlled digestion of parts of the bone-structure. When the dragon died, the control mechanism ceased to operate, and the whole structure corroded. The natives in the passage from Jordanus who went to look for jewels in the body of a fallen dragon found only the skeleton. If they had waited longer they would have found nothing at all. This is why I consider it unlikely that my theory of dragon-flight can ever be proved by the discovery of fossils.

The land about them grew bleak and barren, though once, as Thorin told them, it had been green and fair. There was little grass, and before long there was neither bush nor tree, and only broken and blackened stumps to speak of ones long vanished. They were come to the Desolation of the Dragon, and they were come at the waning of the year.

J. R. R. Tolkien The Hobbit

The Hsia Box (see page 37). In fact the box would have needed to be lined with lead, or more probably gold, to withstand the chemical corrosion of dragon-fluids.

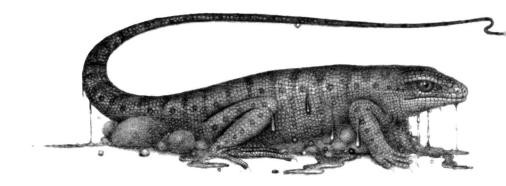

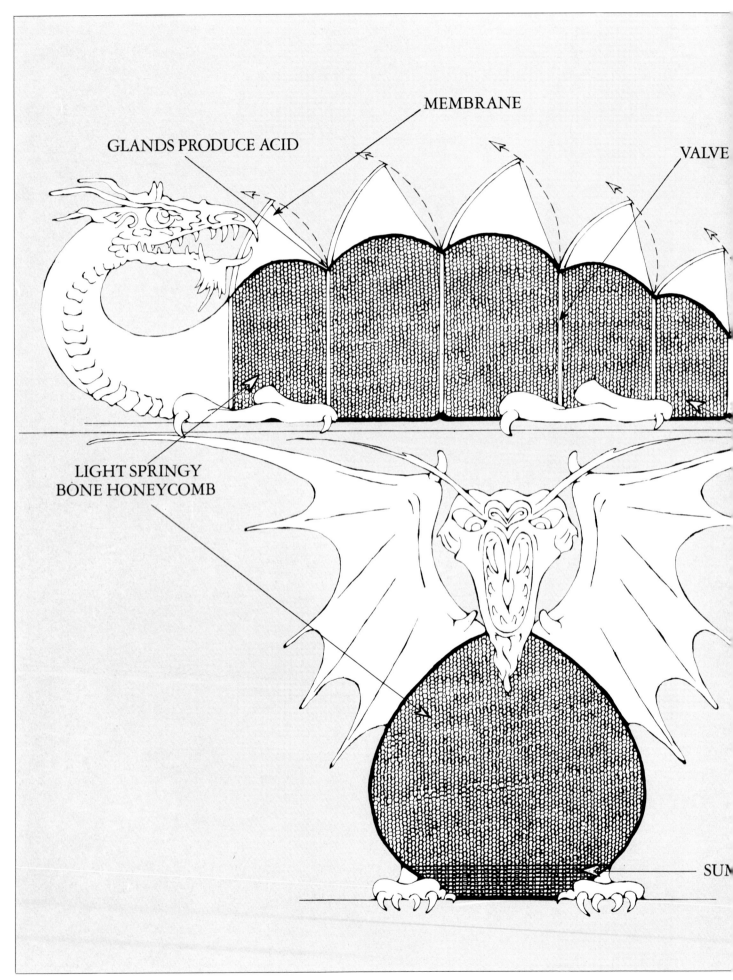

GLANDS PRODUCE ACID

MEMBRANE

VALVE

LIGHT SPRINGY
BONE HONEYCOMB

SUM

42

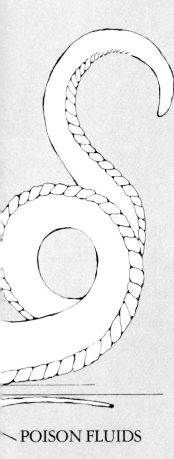

POISON FLUIDS

Flight Cavities

As no fossils are likely to be found, any reconstruction of the dragon's actual body-system is guesswork.

Dragons clearly evolved from lizard-shaped dinosaurs. I envisage cavities which were extreme modifications of the vertebrae of that long spine, each of the selected vertebrae becoming a large, thin-walled urn of bone, closed at the top with a muscular membrane. This membrane, and any other surface needing protection from the acid, would be coated with a resistant mucus, which is the normal way in which digestive systems are prevented from digesting the body they feed. For maximum hydrogen production, the acid gland would open and the acid would flow down the walls of the cavity, reacting with the calcium deposited there from the bone structure. The bone itself would be continually self-renewing.

The various cavities would of course be interconnected by valves, and by adjustment of the tension of the upper membrane transfer of gas throughout the body, for balance and other purposes, could take place. The membranes would have a further vital function. Normally the gas in the cavities would be under mild pressure, and the dragon's weight in air would be positive. It would be light, but it would not actually keep floating upward. For flight, the membranes would relax and the gas volume would expand. The volume of the dragon would increase but its mass would remain the same, so it would become buoyant in air. On a smaller scale a fish's swim-bladder operates in the same way. In fact the dragon when aloft would be swimming in air, rather than flying.

When I say the volume of the dragon increased, this need not have been apparent to the observer, though records of Chinese dragons specifically remark on their ability to vary their size. Another possibility is that the membrane expanded into a space normally filled with air. This would have the same affect as an external increase in volume. A third idea, which I find attractive, is that the great row of "spines" down the dragon's back were not for menace or defence, but were the protective cover for the expanded membranes. When the dragon was at minimum buoyancy they would be laid flat, but were raised for flight.

A system like this would solve a problem about dragon flight which I have not so far mentioned: if the body is long and narrow, but supported solely by the wings, it needs considerable muscular power to maintain itself rigid in the air. But if the body is self-supporting the question does not arise.

EVOLUTION

"Very long ago, as old people have told me, there lived a terrible monster who came out of the North . . . It had a body like an ox, and legs like a frog, two short fore-legs and two long ones behind, and besides that it had a tail like a serpent, ten fathoms in length. When it moved it jumped like a frog, and with every spring it covered half a mile of ground."

The Dragon of the North from *Esthnische Mährchen*

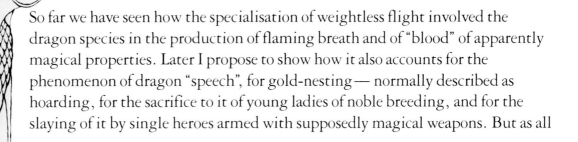

So far we have seen how the specialisation of weightless flight involved the dragon species in the production of flaming breath and of "blood" of apparently magical properties. Later I propose to show how it also accounts for the phenomenon of dragon "speech", for gold-nesting — normally described as hoarding, for the sacrifice to it of young ladies of noble breeding, and for the slaying of it by single heroes armed with supposedly magical weapons. But as all

---

Ummu-Khubur, who formed all things,
. . . has spawned monster-serpents,
Sharp of tooth and cruel of fang;
With poison instead of blood she has filled their bodies.
Fierce monster-vipers she has clothed with terror,
With splendour she has decked them,
She has caused them to mount on high.
Whoever beholds them is overcome by dread.
Their bodies rear up,
None can withstand their attack.

The Babylonian Creation Hymn

these features are connected with the period of its extinction, coinciding with its contact with Man, I will first say something about the evolution of this extraordinary life form, and about its life cycle in its heyday.

Evolution is an erratic process. Some species undergo rapid change, while others remain unaltered through tens of millions of years. There is a blind white fish living in some Mexican caves, and it is possible in this case to show that the fish's ancestors had proper eyes 250,000 years ago and that the final degeneration of the eyes to sightlessness is comparatively recent. This does not mean that every major change must take a quarter of a million years. Some may take longer, some much less. In rare cases even a few generations might suffice.

But there is a curious pattern which tends to repeat itself in quite unrelated species. Slow evolution takes place to a group of simple related forms; a period of stability follows in which these forms do not change; suddenly rapid evolution starts into a lot of very complex forms; and just as suddenly the line is extinct. For instance there is a family of fossils of ammonoid worms which for tens of millions of years were all simple coils in shape; then, as if at a signal, they evolved into loops and braids and double coils and plaits and spirals and pipes; and then they all died out. It is as though they were somehow aware that their time was almost up, and they began searching at random for some unthought-of shape which would allow them to continue to exist.

Dinosaurs followed this pattern. For the first nine-tenths of their rule on earth they kept to simple shapes, clean-limbed, adapted straightforwardly to whatever environment they inhabited. Then came the sudden frenzy of strange shapes, the triple horns, the great ruffs, the frilled and sail-like spinal fins. At the same time came the thrust to adapt to new environments, in particular to the air — the pterosaurs, the dragons and the birds.

As the Cretaceous period drew to its close, all the reptiles with the exception of the crocodiles, the turtles, the lizards and snakes . . . passed into extinction. This mysterious mass death is one of the unsolved riddles in the history of evolution. How could such a variety of animals, many of them giants and at the zenith of their adaptive radiation, disappear so relatively rapidly from the land, the sea and the air . . .?

Kai Petersen Prehistoric Life on Earth

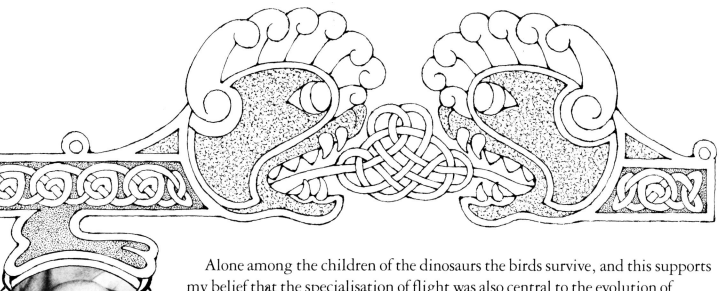

Alone among the children of the dinosaurs the birds survive, and this supports my belief that the specialisation of flight was also central to the evolution of dragons. The birds prove that it was in the air the future of the race lay, and it seems unreasonable to suppose that no other method of flying than with wings and feathers was attempted. Nature, at this stage in the evolutionary process, tries everything, and the history of man's own attempts to fly shows that lighter-than-air methods are simplest, and so likeliest to be successful in the primitive stages of the adventure.

Owing to the absence of fossils it is impossible to trace the stages by which dragons took to the air. (It's worth pointing out though that the same is almost true of birds— all we have are rare finds of two related species of Archeopteryx, and one disputed case of an unrelated species.) But we can produce a plausible set of steps.

At least we can begin with size— something that was already there. Many dinosaurs were very large, for reasons which are still in dispute. Then there

---

Before the dragon has ascended he is of a sort with fish and turtles.
After he has ascended his scales cannot be seen.

The Yuan Kien Lei Han

(*overleaf*) Study of a mythic dragon in flight. Subject unknown, but possibly the dragon Yevaud, in early maturity. This dragon eventually grew to the huge Dragon of Pendor, and as such was mastered by the Wizard Ged, but much earlier, in the days of Elfarrand and Morred, he had spoilt the west of Osskill until he was driven from there by the Wizard Elt, wise in names. (cf Le Guin, *A Wizard of Earthsea*).

Note that though this is clearly a mythic dragon, the artist has retained many features of true dragons. The body appears self-buoyant; the wings are modifications of the rib-cage, thus allowing the creature four legs; the legs themselves, though furnished with formidable-seeming talons, lack musculature; similarly the lower jaw, though ferocious in appearance, has been reduced to fragility to save weight.

Note also the defensive architecture of the island, designed to make landing within the city itself impossible.

appears to have come a time when smaller, quicker creatures were at an advantage. One obvious solution was for the larger species to shrink; some achieved this, but most died out. Another possibility was the retention of size but a reduction in weight; this would make the animal speedier, and at the same time reduce its energy needs. At first simple cavities, and then, once the advantage of lightness had begun to tell, the production of hydrogen. These early steps need not have been dramatic. Small improvements, taking place through many generations, would still have paid off. After all, it is worth filling the tyres of a big modern aeroplane with expensive helium instead of air, just to save weight.

In a period of evolutionary frenzy, such as the one that preceded the extinction of the dinosaurs, any process that has begun tends to go to extremes. While its earthbound fellows were experimenting with horns and frills the proto-dragon was becoming lighter and lighter. Bones became hollow and slight. The armour-like scales of the ancestral dinosaur were discarded, except from the head. We can assume that this ancestor was one of the kangaroo-like big predators which already leaped after its prey, rather than ran. These leaps, as weight decreased, would become more and more dramatic until the half-mile bounds recorded in *The Dragon of the North* were not impossible. (I don't maintain that this is a record of an extant proto-dragon. I think it was more likely an immature male on the verge of flight.) By this stage some form of control of the path of the leap through the air would become essential. The rib-cage would be modified into "wings", and imperceptibly leaping became gliding and gliding became flight.

Dragons could never have been a dominant species; their specialisation carried with it too many disadvantages. But they seem to have achieved a balance, an ecological niche, and like the birds survived the extinction of the dinosaurs. They would never have been creatures of the forests; their bodies were too large and vulnerable, and above all they needed safe cave lairs. They were inevitably inhabitants of cliffs and crags, swooping out to scour the plains for prey among the vast herds of the grass-eaters. The fact that suitable habitats were comparatively few reinforced a trait which was perhaps already there in the ancestral dinosaur— dragons became one of the most territorially possessive species on record. This is something on which all sources agree.

We come now to the section of my theory which I regard as the most

---

He turned to climb out of the valley. He began the climb with a jump and as soon as he jumped he found he was flying.

C. S. Lewis. The Voyage of the Dawntreader

Again after a hundred years Glaurung, the first of the Uroloki, the fire-drakes of the North, issued from Angband's gates by night. He was yet young and scarce half-grown, for long and slow is the life of the dragons, but the Elves fled before him to Ered Wethrin and Dorthonion in dismay; and he defiled the fields of Ard-galen.

J. R. R. Tolkien The Silmarillion

speculative and controversial. I think that female dragons, though they evolved the power of flight along with the males, eventually lost the power and became earthbound again, in fact returned to a semi-aquatic mode of existence. The evidence for this is surprisingly strong, once the possibility has been admitted. First, particularly in the folk-tales, there are countless references to the mothers and grandmothers of dragons being somehow "human". Second, other legends abound with female monsters such as troll-women, which when they are actually described turn out to have too many dragon-traits to be anything else but dragons. Third, all over the world dragons, despite their fiery nature, are associated with pools and water-holes and wells.

It is usually assumed that we are dealing with a number of unrelated species — flying dragons, and swimming dragons, and also the great crawling worms which figure in many of the stories and neither flew nor swam. I think that though there may have been different dragon-species they were all closely similar in habits. By the time Man came on the scene dragons had evolved to a life cycle in which the mature males could fly, the immature males were not yet big enough to achieve the necessary lift, and the females remained in and near the ancestral water.

The reasons for this further stage of evolution can in fact be guessed at. The

---

The troll-woman was a huge monster, livid as Hel and large as a bull; behind, she was a snake with a fish-tail attached. She yawned terribly with her maw, and her teeth jutted far out in front of her, and poison and sparks flew afar from her jaws; the poison gushed out plentifully over Hogni and his companions.

Andra Saga Jarls

We consider that Dragons do not readily perish from hunger; for we read in a volume of natural history that these beasts can easily endure starvation. But when afterwards, they indulge their stomachs, Dragons are insatiable.   Ulysses Aldrovandus

dragons took to the air and so survived whatever ecological crisis it was that caused the extinction of the dinosaurs. When the crisis had passed there was no real need to continue flight—the disadvantages of the lighter-than-air body would now show up in competition with the much more efficient birds. But in the meanwhile the need for suitable habitats had imposed a life cycle on the dragons which I will describe in the next section. Territorial possessiveness had been reinforced to a stage where the mating-grounds were "owned" by the most successful males, and this success was measured by the ability to fly and to breathe fire. So, though there was no longer a need for flight in order for the individual animal to survive, it was still needed for the species as a whole to reproduce. One sees a similar phenomenon in many extant species, where the most distinctive adaptation of the male—the tail of the bird of paradise, for instance, or the curious buttocks of the mandrill—is there solely to attract the female or to assert dominance for mating purposes.

The female had no such need, and every reason to abandon the serious disadvantages of the flight-mechanism—bulk and conspicuousness and vulnerability. Pools and creeks provided a more available and safer habitat, especially as there was no question of sharing a lair with an animal of such a tricky temperament as the male dragon. So the female returned to the water and at the same time became a more reasonable size. Certain dragon-traits inevitably

---

Moreover we have recent witness in the History of the expedition to Florida, where a winged serpent was seen, and slain not far from a wood. Its wings were so small that they could scarcely raise the animal from the ground. Furthermore the Christians observed that the natives took great trouble to remove the head of the dead beast; which they deduced was done because of some superstition.

Ulysses Aldrovandus Historia Serpentium et Draconum

When a species goes in for sexual display it affects many aspects of behaviour. The extreme example, the bird of paradise, does not merely grow exotic plumage to attract the female and then rely on that. It adds both dance and song to its armoury. Some species of this bird clear special areas to dance on, and decorate them with flowers and bright objects. Others display on trees, dangling upside-down on branches and emitting an extraordinary variety of calls.

A species as exotic as the dragon would have behaved analogously, both in combat with rival males and in courtship of the female. The more extraordinary the behaviour-patterns one can imagine, the more likely they are to be true.

remained — the poisonous metabolism, the ability to spit sparks at least, if not great gouts of flame, the hideous look, and the upright gait when not alarmed.

It is this last feature, inherited from the ancestral dinosaur, which accounts for the folk-tales about dragons having human mothers and grandmothers. To simple people the distinguishing mark of Man is not reason, or tools, or speech, but the ability to walk on his hind legs. Confronted by an enemy the male dragon, if it did not take refuge in flight, would keep its vulnerable underside close to the ground. But the female, whose protective rib-cage had not been modified into "wings", would be more likely to remain upright waving short, taloned fore-limbs not unlike arms. There is a particularly good account in *Beowulf* of how human and yet not-human such a creature must have seemed to the observer.

Aldrovandus and Jordanus
I have used several quotations from "The Natural History of Dragons" by Ulysses Aldrovandus, and one from "The Wonders of the East" by Jordanus. These were two quite different kinds of writer. Aldrovandus was a stay-at-home scholar who wrote a many-volumed "Natural History" in Bologna in the early part of the 17th Century. The section on dragons occupies only half a volume (compared with a whole volume devoted to poultry). Later writers on dragons refer to him with barely-concealed mockery as a credulous collector of nonsense, but this is unfair. He does his best to distinguish fancy from genuine tradition, and though he may print an engraving of a monster which is clearly a manta ray with an

54

ape's head sewn on to it, in his text he makes it clear that he knows it is a fake.

On the other hand I myself have been unfair to Jordanus, who was no stay-at-home scholar but a brave travelling priest who wrote bad Latin. In his little book, written but not published three centuries before Aldrovandus, he describes his journey to India, and what he saw and heard there. He invents nothing. All his personal observations are clearly accurate; if he visits an area of no interest he says so, and does not people it with monsters; and he distinguishes between what he has seen and what he has been told. The important quotation on page 27 is something he was told, and though it is still obviously the product of an often-repeated tradition, Jordanus reports it with the immediacy of an oral legend, before the European scholars had had time to tamper with it.

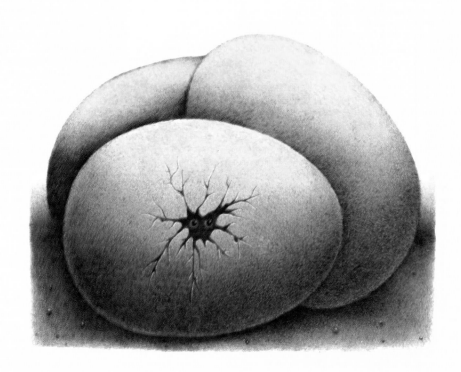

LIFE CYCLE

"He took a long drink and then . . . he ate nearly all the dead dragon. . . . There is nothing a dragon likes so well as fresh dragon. That is why you so seldom find more than one dragon in the same country."

C. S. Lewis *The Voyage of the Dawn Treader*

NOTE: I have written this section as fiction. This is not because I think it any less credible than the rest of this book, but because it is grammatically convenient. The life cycle I describe is a reasonable one and fits in with all the facts we know, but particularly in detail other suggestions are just as plausible. By using fiction I am simply avoiding all the "woulds" and "mights" which would otherwise speckle the story.

It begins and ends with an egg. A she-dragon comes heavily out of the desert night to the watering hole. She drinks, then squats for a while by the pool and lays three eggs, over which she scrapes a low mound of earth and dead scrub. She warbles to herself all the while as she does this. Far off, to the north, over the mountains, a streak of flame shows for a moment against the stars, where the old male dragon is still asserting his right to the mating-pool. She answers the signal with a croaking cry and continues her work. When it is done she rears onto her hind legs and waddles away, still warbling.

In the hills there is a pool where a bad dragon lives; long ago some merchants rested by the pool, until the dragon became enraged, abused and killed them.

There are self-existent dragons and there are worms that are changed into dragons.

The Kiao belongs to the Dragon species . . . he is hidden in the streams and his eggs are opened at the mound.
The Yuan Kien Lei Han

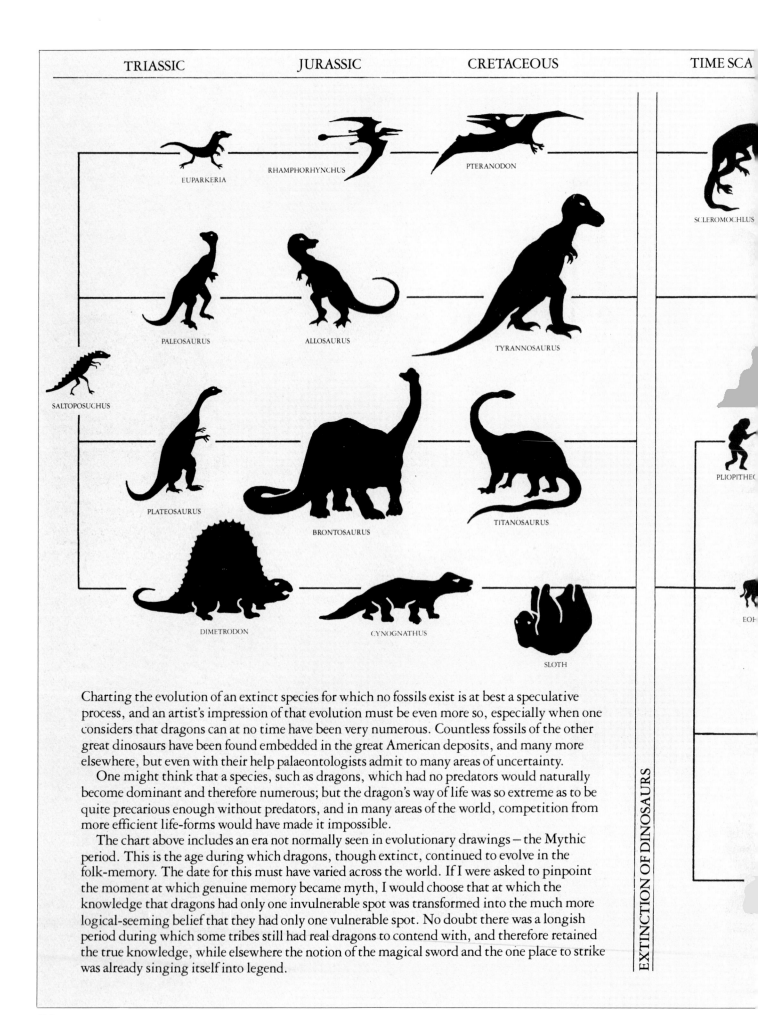

Charting the evolution of an extinct species for which no fossils exist is at best a speculative process, and an artist's impression of that evolution must be even more so, especially when one considers that dragons can at no time have been very numerous. Countless fossils of the other great dinosaurs have been found embedded in the great American deposits, and many more elsewhere, but even with their help palaeontologists admit to many areas of uncertainty.

One might think that a species, such as dragons, which had no predators would naturally become dominant and therefore numerous; but the dragon's way of life was so extreme as to be quite precarious enough without predators, and in many areas of the world, competition from more efficient life-forms would have made it impossible.

The chart above includes an era not normally seen in evolutionary drawings – the Mythic period. This is the age during which dragons, though extinct, continued to evolve in the folk-memory. The date for this must have varied across the world. If I were asked to pinpoint the moment at which genuine memory became myth, I would choose that at which the knowledge that dragons had only one invulnerable spot was transformed into the much more logical-seeming belief that they had only one vulnerable spot. No doubt there was a longish period during which some tribes still had real dragons to contend with, and therefore retained the true knowledge, while elsewhere the notion of the magical sword and the one place to strike was already singing itself into legend.

EXTINCTION OF DINOSAURS

PROAVIS

ARCHAEOPTERYX

COMMON CROW

CON

PTERODRACON

PSEUDODRACON

MYTHODRACON

HECUS

AUSTRALOPITHECUS

NEANDERTHAL MAN

CRO-MAGNON MAN

MESOHIPPUS

MERYCHIPPOS

EQUUS

MAMMOTH

MODERN ELEPHANT

TOOTH TIGER

TIGER

EXTINCTION OF DRAGONS

The egg under its mound is as large as two clenched fists. Its shell is smooth and hard as fine porcelain, but slowly, as the life inside its stirs and grows, chemical juices are released. The inner surface softens and is absorbed into the developing body, until the shell is brittle and thin. Sensing its hour, the thing inside heaves. The shell cracks.

A little troop of eohippus are drinking at the pool in the moonlight. Their sentry startles at a movement of the earth, and all heads turn to watch the mound erupt. They see a dark slim shape wriggle out of the earth and slither into the pool. Unflurried they return to their drinking.

Safe in the water the tiny horror licks from its sides the remnants of shell— the start of a life-long habit of eating calcium-containing substances. It rests, and then begins to browse among the pondweed. At this stage it has a ruff of external gills along either side of the neck, and rudimentary legs. It is six inches long and looks like a large newt. Only the wide, characteristic dragon-mask distinguishes it from other lizards. Before dawn it is joined by a brother, and next night by the inmate of the last of the three eggs, a female— darker in colour, broader across

---

The young heir of Lambton took up the gruesome thing, and, taking it off his hook, cast it into a well close by, and ever since that day that well has gone by the name of Worm Well.

For some time nothing more was seen or heard of the Worm, till one day it had outgrown the size of the well, and came forth full-grown. So it came forth and betook itself to the Wear. And all day long it would lie coiled on a rock in the middle of the stream, while at night it came forth from the river and harried the country-side.

The Lambton Worm

Clearly a mythic scene. The maturity of the vegetation alone proves that this was not regular dragon country. This makes it all the more significant that the association of dragon-hatching with water should remain so strong in the subconscious mind.

The detail of the "nostrils" raises a point. The venting of fire would demand heavily protected orifices; the probable need to keep the inflammable gases separate from oxygen until they were clear of the body might actually have led to the evolution of quite separate channels for fiery "breath" and true breath. In that case the real nostrils would be much smaller and to all intents unnoticeable.

the body and with a less pronounced tail.

For two whole years the three of them live their newt-life, growing steadily. Their appetite increases until the pondweed can no longer keep pace with it, and at this point a common natural mechanism takes over. The female is basking near the surface, a fish-like shape almost two feet long, when with no warning or signal at all the two males home in on her. There is a brief wild flurry in the water, first as they kill her and then as they fight for her body. Our dragon, slightly the stronger of the two, wins the larger pieces and so increases his own advantage in size and strength. A few weeks later there is only one baby dragon in the pond.

(Elsewhere, in broad stretches of breeding water such as the Beowulf Mere, the mechanism is not triggered because the dragon-young are able to disperse, so the cannibalistic stage takes place much later, as a part of the process of territorial aggressiveness.)

Now the pondweed has time to regenerate for a while, but already the chemistry of the dragon-metabolism is beginning to operate. Many travellers have remarked on the stillness and blackness of the water in dragon-pools. Shortly the water becomes too acid for vegetation, and as for animal life, the dragon has acquired the taste for flesh. In the end the eohippus learn to go elsewhere for their drinking.

This stage again takes several years, and then a further change begins and the dragon emerges from the water to hunt on land. By this time he is nine or ten feet long, of a mottled slimy green colour above, and paler below. If you happened to come on him without his being aware of you, you would see a creature crouched up on its hind legs and balancing against its tail. Down the long flank below the curiously human forearms you might notice fold on fold of ridged membrane, where the rib-cage was already starting to grow into "wings". But you would not be likely to pay any attention to these details, because your eye would be held by the head — strangely too large for the body, with big yellow forward-facing eyes — the dragon-mask. As soon as the animal was aware of your presence (and its smell and hearing were very acute) it would drop to the ground, protecting its vulnerable underside, and look at you. If it decided you were dangerous it might begin to retreat, shuffling away backwards. But if it thought you were food, it would come towards you, slowly, staring all the time. You would need a strong will to break away from the stare, to see anything else but the steadily advancing head, to force your numb limbs into action, to turn, to run . . .

If you made it, the dragon would not run after you.

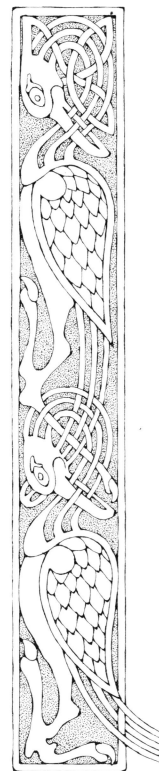

For a while the dragon hunts close by his old pool, living on small prey as he becomes used to the appalling pull of gravity after the weightlessness of his body in water. Insofar as an animal can be conscious of such things, the whole of the next stage of his development is a time of deep anxiety and danger, and also of depression — it is a long age between the safety and buoyancy of water and the safety and buoyancy of air. In order to achieve the incredible reduction of mass, he has to become both huge and vulnerable. The process is going to take years, and if he is to survive them he must find a safe lair.

The fluid has long ago drained from the rudimentary flight-cavities in his body. The big one below the neck is already beginning to fill with gas. A season comes when he is ready to trek towards the mountains and begin his search. He must find a cave of a special sort, long enough to contain his full-grown body, narrow enough to be defended by his head. The cave must be in limestone country, where the streams are rich in calcium. Luckily limestone country tends to be full of caves — and he needs to be lucky. Of the several hundred eggs laid in the same year as his, some forty males still survive and four females. Being smaller, the females tend to get eaten first. But now the balance is about to be redressed. Of these four females, three will live to lay fertile eggs. Of the forty males, only two will ever join the mating-flights, and of all the males born in his year and the year before his and the three years after, only he will actually mate.

The appalling death rate is the price of specialisation. The dragon body, apart from the flight-cavities, has a basic weight. Head, lungs, heart, guts, muscles, bones, skin, wings — from the start they all weigh something, however brittle the hollow bones may be, however slowly the creature moves to avoid the build-up of muscle. The flight-cavities also have weight, but this is counteracted

Often I wish I had not eaten my wife
(Though worm grows not to dragon till he eats worm).
She could have helped me, watch and watch about,
Guarding the gold; the gold would have been safer.

C. S. Lewis The Pilgrim's Regress

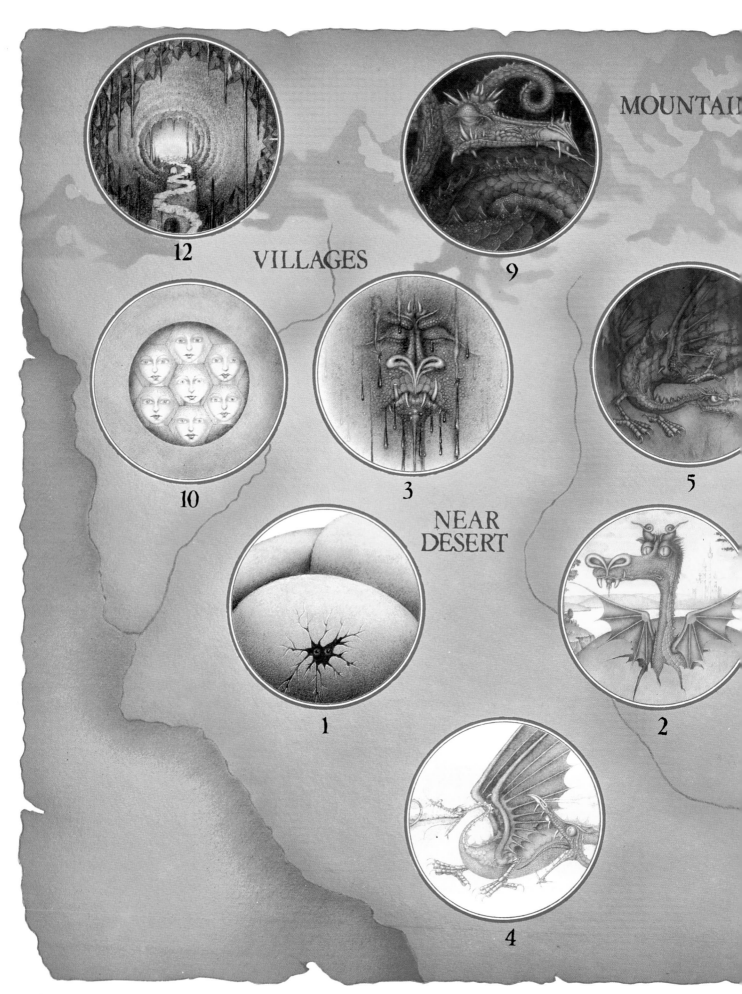

MOUNTAIN

VILLAGES

NEAR
DESERT

12

9

10

3

5

1

2

4

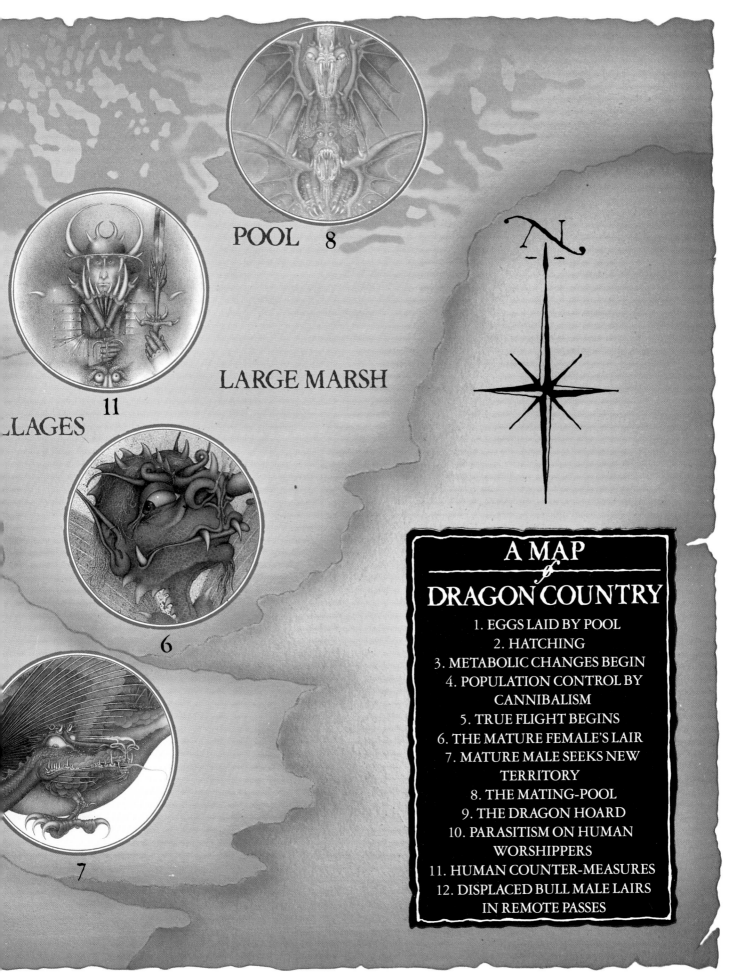

POOL   8

11

LLAGES

LARGE MARSH

N

6

7

A MAP
of
DRAGON COUNTRY
1. EGGS LAID BY POOL
2. HATCHING
3. METABOLIC CHANGES BEGIN
4. POPULATION CONTROL BY
CANNIBALISM
5. TRUE FLIGHT BEGINS
6. THE MATURE FEMALE'S LAIR
7. MATURE MALE SEEKS NEW
TERRITORY
8. THE MATING-POOL
9. THE DRAGON HOARD
10. PARASITISM ON HUMAN
WORSHIPPERS
11. HUMAN COUNTER-MEASURES
12. DISPLACED BULL MALE LAIRS
IN REMOTE PASSES

by the gas within them, so that they each have a certain amount of lift. When the dragon has grown enough cavities they will each be able to lift their share of the basic weight — provided that hasn't increased in the meanwhile — and the whole creature will fly.

The process takes nearly thirty years. Each winter he hibernates. Each summer he grows, with painful speed, a fresh flight-cavity. Even in summer he has to be sluggish — he cannot afford the muscle for swift movement, because muscle is weight. Nor can he afford the armour for protection against attack, because bone and scales are weight too. Only his head is almost invulnerable; he uses his hypnotic stare both to hunt prey and to concentrate the attacks of his enemies onto the one part of him that is not vulnerable. (In fact he is more vulnerable to sharp edges than to solid blows; his hide will yield to a buffet or a flung stone, but can be pierced by a fang or a talon.)

So, having found his lair — having found in fact a long narrow cleft at the foot of a cliff and eaten the body of its previous occupant who had very recently crawled back there and died after failing to hypnotise an angry sabre-tooth — our dragon lives through the hell of his long adolescence. He spends all the time he can in his cave, but occasionally he is forced out to hunt — though as most of his body is neither flesh nor blood he needs far less food than any animal of comparable size. A wild pig will last him a month. On these expeditions he is a crawling worm, slow and monstrous, giving an impression of invincible weight. To catch prey he lies in ambush, waiting for a suitable animal to move within range of his stare and be caught. He drinks from a safe pool.

After a while the water in the streams and the bones of his prey are no longer enough to provide the calcium he needs, and he takes to swallowing rocks and small boulders for the additional limestone. The process quickens. The flight-cavities, which for years have been only partially filled with hydrogen to reduce the need for weight and hence for muscle, begin to fill completely. The leg muscles partially atrophy, but the wing muscles build up. Windless evenings bring him out, full of vague longings and frustrations, even when he is not hungry. He rears up on his hind legs and rattles his spread wings. He springs upward, and for a moment he is almost flying.

These leaps continue, and increase. Instinct controls the flexing of the membranes over the flight-cavities, opens and closes the connecting valves, steadies his posture in the air. He practises the use of his wings as he swoops through the dusk, and learns to use them for safe landings, though being almost weightless a fall will hardly hurt him, unless he's unlucky enough to split himself on a sharp ridge. And then, one warm evening, a leap takes him into the remains of a desert thermal and sweeps him skyward. The apparently huge bulk lurches,

---

Anyone who had the ill luck to look into those eyes became as it were bewitched and was obliged to rush of his own accord into the monster's jaws. In this way the Dragon was able to feed upon both men and beasts without the least trouble to itself, as it needed not to move from the spot where it was lying.

The Dragon of the North

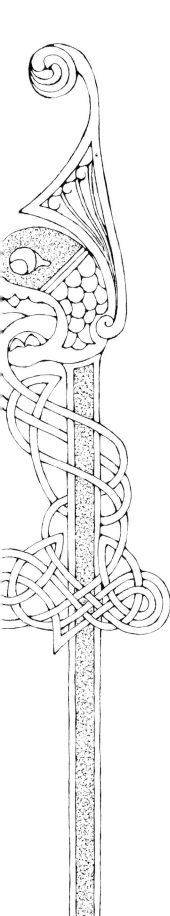

wavers, wobbles into a downdraught and rushes towards the rocks. Panic stimulates the membranes to stretch still further; glands squirt acid down the walls of the flight-cavities. The downrush ceases, he wavers into still air and there begins to float gently up, higher and higher, flying at last.

But in the panic and struggle he has over-produced hydrogen, so that even when the membranes are contracted to maximum pressure he is still buoyant. Again instinct answers. Valves open, and a jet of hydrogen flows up the gullet, through the jaws. Six inches beyond the gaping snout it bellows into flame, a long plume, flaring against the dusk. And now, far off beyond cliff and crag, an old dragon wandering down the night wind sees the signal and answers with his own roaring jet — not a welcome, but a challenge, a recognition that a new dragon is flying, a rival who will soon be coming to fight for the mating-grounds.

For the first time since he left the pool where he was hatched our dragon is safe and free again. He is part of an element. He begins to learn the pathways of the wind, the lines of thermals that stretch across the plain and help him to hunt the great herds that forage there. He can even, if he wishes, explore the mountain range for a better and safer lair. In fact his own lair is good enough — that is why he alone of his brood has survived so long.

These first flights take place in the late summer, after he has grown the last essential cavity. All the autumn he hunts and feeds, and when winter rules the plain and the herds go south he hibernates. In the spring he comes out to hunt again, growing stronger and surer every day — every fine day, that is. Even the oldest and most experienced dragon keeps to his cave in storm-time, because bodies as light as theirs are helpless when anything more than a gentle wind is up. In areas where the winds are steady and predictable they learn to ride them and use them, but in storm-gusts they are whirled along like blown leaves.

But all through this season he has felt a new urge, calling him towards a centre. Night after night the signals have increased, the flame-flares challenging and answering for a hundred miles and more along the great escarpment. At first they are random, but soon they acquire a focus. They gather to a point, a circling fire-dance. To that point our dragon comes also. Being the youngest he reaches it last of all.

The Phrygian History also states that dragons are born which reach ten paces in length; which daily . . . are wont to proceed from their caverns, and (near the river Rhyndacus), with part of the body on the ground and the rest erect, with the neck gently stretched out, and gaping mouth, attract birds, either by their inspiration, or by some fascination, and that those which are drawn down by the inhalation of their breath glide down into their stomach.

Aelian De Natura Animalium

He finds about twenty of his kind circling over a dark tarn where the foothills surge up into the true mountains. All the area below is barren rock, poisoned by generations of dragon-juices. The dragons wheel above in spiralling flight, the circles narrowing and narrowing until they close to a point directly above the tarn. That point is the station of the old bull-dragon who "owns" the tarn, and the dragon directly below is challenging him for it, while those below are working their way up the spiral in a whole series of individual fights until they earn the right to be the next challenger. Our dragon swings into the dance at the outer edge. All night he circles there, breathing very little flame, only venturing into two inconclusive encounters with other young dragons. But at the peak of the cone the fight is real. There the old bull and his challenger are circling close, snorting their fifty-yard plumes of fire, singed here and there with the jets from their rival's gullet, manoeuvring for the upper hand. "Upper" in a quite literal sense, because with each spout of flame the fighters lose lift, and the contest is really to see which of them can rise higher and still breathe fire, which can hover flaring above his flameless rival and force him to earth. That dragon will be the

best flier in the dance. He will have proved that his genes are the most suitable to be passed on to the next generation of dragons. This time the old bull wins, and the challenger glides down into a lower circle — his turn may come again.

Three nights later the old bull is beaten. In a final effort to assert his power he belches out more gas than he can spare, loses lift, begins to glide down, but on the way passes close by our dragon. The instinct to fight, the call of the tarn, is stronger even than the instinct for survival. Another vast plume of fire gushes out, and as our dragon breathes his feeble answer the old bull's glide steepens disastrously and he hurls down into the crags. His cavity-membranes are already extended to their utmost, and the sudden pressure of impact is too much for them. He literally bursts apart, while above him the dance goes on.

These fire-dances last only a fortnight or so before the dragons disperse, leaving the new bull to rule his tarn. The year becomes like last year for our

dragon, except that he grows another cavity, learns to fly higher and more skilfully, and can breathe stronger fire. Then he hibernates, and another year follows, and another set of dances. So year after year he grows, and year after year he fights his way higher up the spiral until at last he is the challenger at the central point, circling the bull-dragon, higher and higher. He breathes a short spurt of flame and seems for a moment to stagger in the air, but as the old bull closes he uses the momentum of that minor swoop to swing himself up and round, so close that the thin wings rattle against each other. The feint has caught the old bull unawares, and as if it were a rehearsed movement of the dance, our dragon is suddenly above, an inverse shadow, following every move, talons stretched to pierce the fragile body below if the old bull tries to rise any further. The bull's response is flame, not directed at his enemy, but flame as pure display. Jet for jet his rival answers him. In both their innards the glands squirt fresh acid down the endlessly consumed honeycomb of bone which is the inner surface of the flight-cavities, but our dragon is younger, the bone-structure newer, the channels which replace the calcium less exhausted. Suddenly the old dragon has no more gas to give and glides away, clear out of the dance. He never returns, but flies north, far away, finds a fresh lair and becomes one of those morose and treacherous old dragons which haunt the mountain passes.

Now our dragon is bull. He holds his position until the dances are ended and the other males disperse, leaving him master of the tarn. He perches on a sentinel crag, renewing his energies.

Meanwhile, all over the plain, the season has stirred the hormones of the females, altering their chemistry, forcing them out of pool and mere to lie for a

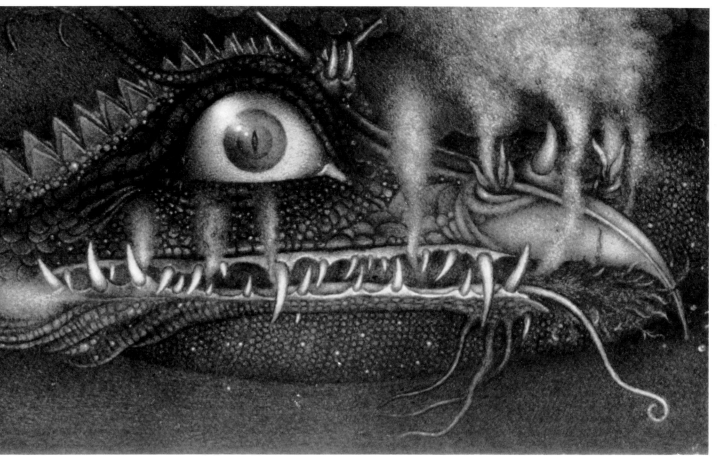

while and become accustomed to this other element. From their own rudimentary cavities the fluids drain, lightening them for their journey to the mountains. They rear up on their hind legs and waddle clumsily north by night, their eyes on the fire-dance that flickers above the cliffs. At each jet of flame they give their strange warbling cry. The journey for even the nearest takes several days, and for some almost a month, and if two of them meet as they near the tarn they fight with serious ferocity to establish precedence. In all there are nearly eighty who come to the tarn, the youngest around ten years old and the oldest around thirty, whereas our dragon is by now at least fifty years old. The fights and the different distances have the effect of spacing the arrivals out, four at most in a night.

A particular female comes waddling between the rocks and waits at the water's edge, her eyes on the starry darkness above. The tarn is still. Suddenly between the stars a streak of flame grows, widens and is gone. She answers with a cry — the same warbling note which she has been giving during her journey but

---

Why the future Foreign Secretary should leave a bell-jar full of hair-streak caterpillars in my bedroom I do not remember. I didn't mind at the time. There were about sixty of them, feeding placidly on the leaves of the shrubs he had found them on, and they clearly couldn't get out of the bell-jar. I slept well, without nightmares. If I woke in the night I heard no tiny screams, no scrunching. But when I woke in the morning and looked at the jar I found that there were only three caterpillars left, all appreciably larger than they had been the night before. As I stared, two of the survivors began to breakfast on the third.

Peter Dickinson Autobiography

magnified a hundred times so that it is a wavering scream that echoes among the crags — and slips into the water. As she swims a third of her body, buoyed by the drained cavities, lies clear of the silky surface, so that the dragon, swooping down in answer to her cry, sees it as a moving patch of pure black among the reflected stars. He flames again, she cries in answer and he closes down on her.

Like everything else in the dragon's life, it is a violent mating. His talons close on her neck and haunches. His wings spread for balance as she writhes beneath him. Foam and spray flash in the starlight, swirling into steam where the water-drops catch his flaming breath. The rocks re-echo with their screams.

Violent and brief. Now he rises heavily into the air, clutches at his sentinel-crag and rests, while she floats as if dead on the now-still tarn with the dark blood from her torn flanks drifting into misty patterns around her. After a while she swims to the shore and drags herself out. Close by there is a new-come female, squatting patiently on the rocks, staring at the sky as she waits for the signal, but neither pays any attention to the other. Slowly the mated female journeys to her own jealously guarded district, where she visits all her laying-sites in turn, leaving two or three eggs at each and covering them carefully with sand or rotten weeds. It makes no difference to her that in most of these waters there is already a half-grown dragon in possession which will eagerly gobble up her new-hatched young as they slither into the water. There are still perhaps two or three pools which have lost their occupants since the previous year, and that will be enough to begin the cycle again.

The dragons begin to speak. Ying and Yang are commingled.

The Yuan Kien Lei Han

The male cries above and the female cries below and he changes.

The Yuan Kien Lei Han

Dragon Sightings in Britain

1) DORNOCH. Dragon attacked town, was killed by St Gilbert with an arrow.

2) LOCH NESS. Clearly an ancestral breeding-mere.

3) BEN VAIR. Dragon preyed on travellers using Ballachulish crossing. Killed by spike-covered raft baited with meat.

4) KIRKTON OF STRATHMARTINE. Dragon ate girls using well. Killed by young peasant with club.

5) LINTON. Dragon ravaged farms. Killed by fire-ball attached to end of lance and thrust down throat.

6) LONGWITTON. Invisible dragon lurked near well. Knight used magic ointment to see it, killed it after luring it from water.

7) SPINDLESTON HEUGH. The Laidly Worm (loathsome dragon) lived in a cave and poisoned the countryside. Was in fact a maiden transformed by sorcery, and rescued by her brother who had come to kill her but was persuaded to kiss her instead.

8) BISHOP'S AUCKLAND. Pollard of Pollard Hall killed a dragon in an oak-wood. His descendants had to present the falchion he used to each new Bishop of Durham to prove their right to their land.

9) LAMBTON. Heir of Lambton fished a vile worm out of the river and threw it into a well, where it grew to a dragon. He returned from foreign parts to kill it, using spiked armour.

10) SEXHOW. Dragon in woods, killed by farmer and his dog.

11) WELL. Dragon in Well, killed by young man in spiked barrel.

12) NUNNINGTON. Poisonous, self-healing dragon killed by knight in armour covered with razors. Helped by dog.

13) FILEY. Dragon in gulley on seashore. Killed by being given sticky cake which glued jaws together while villagers attacked it.

14) WANTLEY. Dragon lived in wood by well. Killed by More of More Hall, in spiked armour, who kicked dragon in one vulnerable spot after two-day battle.

15) ANWICK. Dragon guarded treasure under immovable stone.

16) PENMYNNEDD. Dragon killed by being lured into pit containing bronze mirror. Exhausted itself fighting own reflection.

17) DENBIGH. Dragon devastated country. Killed by knight with two thumbs on each hand.

18) LLANRHAEDR-YM-MOCHANT. Dragon killed by wrapping itself round stone studded with spikes and then draped with red cloth.

19) LLANDEILO GRABAN. Dragon roosted on church tower. Killed by wooden dummy set with sharp hooks.

20) BROMFIELD. Dragon overcome by spells of Saracen sorcerer. Huge treasure hoard found.

21) BRINSOP. St George killed a well-dwelling dragon.

22) MORDIFORD. Several dragons reported, one killed by a knight, one by a band of villagers, and one or more by barrels set with spikes.

23) DEERHURST. Poisonous, man-eating dragon killed while sleeping.

24) CHIPPING NORTON. Visited in 1349 by two-headed, bat-winged beast.

25) UFFINGTON. St George killed a dragon.

26) BRENT PELHAM. The devil demanded the soul of a knight who had killed a dragon, but he was saved by being buried half in and half out of holy ground.

27) WORMESGAY. One-eyed dragon killed by knight after intervention of St Guthlac, who dazzled the monster with a lightning flash, enabling knight to reach one invulnerable spot (a wart).

28) LUDHAM. Nocturnal dragon laired in cellars of ruined abbey.

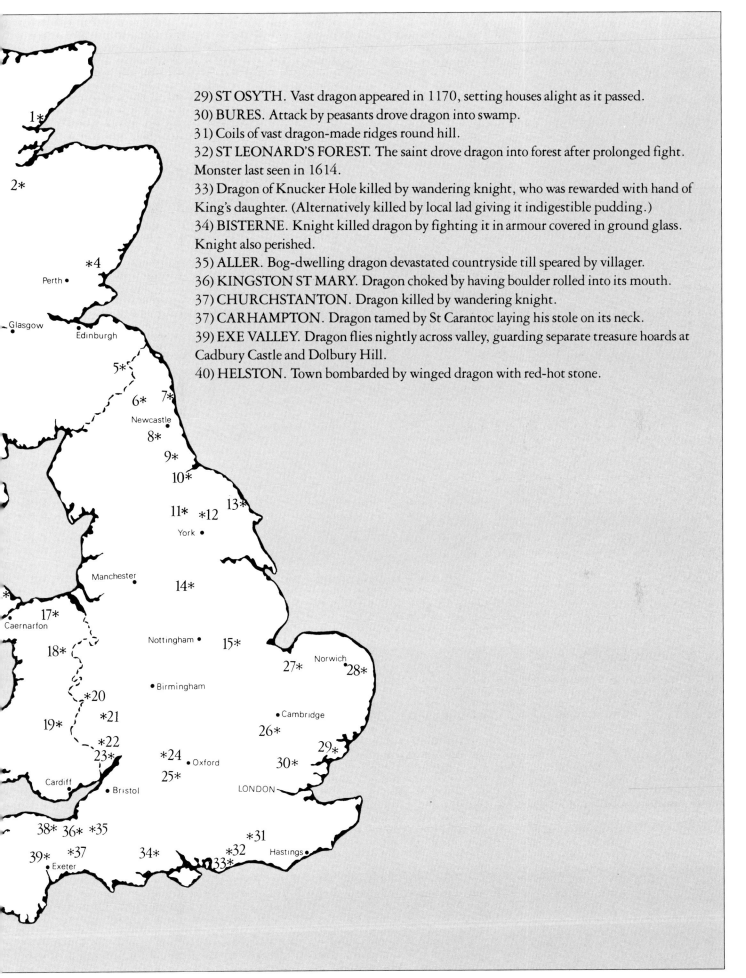

29) ST OSYTH. Vast dragon appeared in 1170, setting houses alight as it passed.

30) BURES. Attack by peasants drove dragon into swamp.

31) Coils of vast dragon-made ridges round hill.

32) ST LEONARD'S FOREST. The saint drove dragon into forest after prolonged fight. Monster last seen in 1614.

33) Dragon of Knucker Hole killed by wandering knight, who was rewarded with hand of King's daughter. (Alternatively killed by local lad giving it indigestible pudding.)

34) BISTERNE. Knight killed dragon by fighting it in armour covered in ground glass. Knight also perished.

35) ALLER. Bog-dwelling dragon devastated countryside till speared by villager.

36) KINGSTON ST MARY. Dragon choked by having boulder rolled into its mouth.

37) CHURCHSTANTON. Dragon killed by wandering knight.

37) CARHAMPTON. Dragon tamed by St Carantoc laying his stole on its neck.

39) EXE VALLEY. Dragon flies nightly across valley, guarding separate treasure hoards at Cadbury Castle and Dolbury Hill.

40) HELSTON. Town bombarded by winged dragon with red-hot stone.

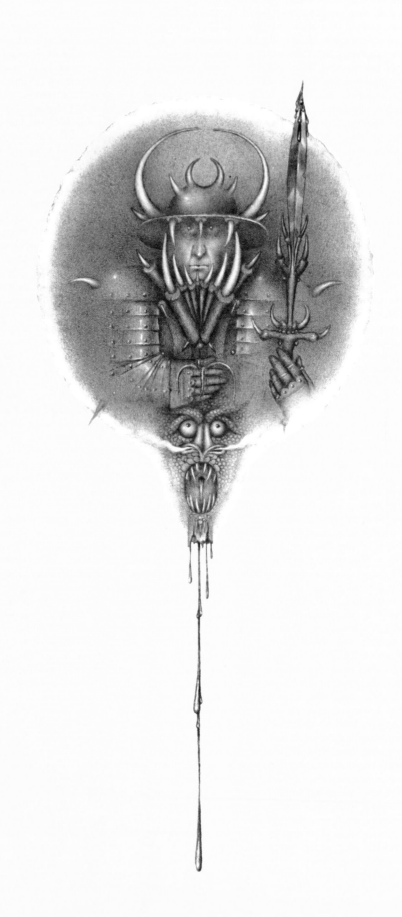

THE HERO WITH THE SWORD

> "Why didst thou leave the trodden paths of men
> Too soon, and with weak hands though mighty heart
> Dare the unpastured dragon in his den?
> Defenceless as thou wert, oh, where was then
> Wisdom the mirrored shield, or scorn the spear?"

Shelley *Adonais*

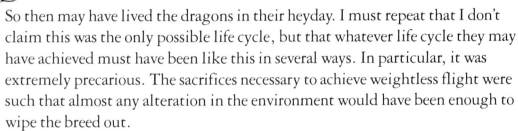

So then may have lived the dragons in their heyday. I must repeat that I don't claim this was the only possible life cycle, but that whatever life cycle they may have achieved must have been like this in several ways. In particular, it was extremely precarious. The sacrifices necessary to achieve weightless flight were such that almost any alteration in the environment would have been enough to wipe the breed out.

Chief of these sacrifices was the acceptance of extreme vulnerability. I cannot emphasise this enough. Suppose we recalculate the weight of the dragon Orm Embar in the light of what we have since discovered. When I did the original sums on page 20 I was concerned to minimise the animal's volume, in order to save mass. Now I am concerned to maximise volume in order to provide lift. If we increase his maximum diameter from 6 ft. to 9 ft., and allow his whole body to taper less sharply at either end, then we can achieve a reasonable volume around 4000 cubic feet. Let us assume that the "wings" are sufficiently aerodynamic to lift their own weight. 4000 cubic feet of gas will lift 280 lb., a weight roughly equivalent to a very large man, or between four and five cubic feet of normal flesh and bone. Assume all the weight-saving strategies

The dragons of all countries must be propitiated by human sacrifice, commonly of a virgin princess.

Larousse Encyclopedia of Mythology

conceivable, and it might be possible to double the volume of solid matter distributed through the whole vast body of the dragon, but however it is arranged, it is going to be very thin almost everywhere.

This vulnerability would be protected in a number of ways. First, by the ability to fly; second, by extreme wariness, amounting to timidity in most situations; third, by an appearance of monstrous ferocity allied with the hypnotic powers (which I have already mentioned and about which I will have more to say later); fourth, by the weapon of fiery breath; fifth, by the habit of lairing in narrow caves; sixth, by what I have hitherto called the dragon-mask, the corky mass of nerveless tissue which protected the true skull and absorbed the attacks which the hypnotic stare concentrated there; seventh, by being inedible, except by other dragons, and eighth, by the nature of the body-structure itself.

Being mostly composed of inflated membrane, the body was vulnerable to some forms of attack more than others. It was highly flexible, and unless distended to its pressure-limit could absorb quite heavy blows and buffets. Very few other creatures would have any reason to attack it, and those that did would either concentrate on the invulnerable head, or else find themselves unable to open their jaws wide enough to bite at the yielding curve of membrane along the flanks. On the other hand an attacker with tusks or sharp talons would be a real danger — perhaps the tradition of enmity between dragons and elephants harks back to this fact.

So somehow the dragons survived, never in very great numbers and always in particular areas where suitable lairs were available. Many changes must indeed have happened in the biosphere, and often no doubt the breeding numbers were reduced to dangerously few; but always they managed to recover until the final fatal change occurred. This was no upheaval of land masses, no creeping south of

---

. . . in the very midst of their talk a tall figure stepped from the shadows. He was drenched with water, his black hair hung wet over his face, and a fierce light was in his eyes.

"Bard is not lost!" he cried. "He dived from Esgaroth, when the enemy was slain. I am Bard, of the line of Girion; I am the slayer of the dragon!"

"King Bard! King Bard!" they shouted.

J. R. R. Tolkien The Hobbit

glaciers, no alteration of the sun — the dragons had seen and endured all those — but the coming of a new enemy, a ferocious ape, hunting in packs, cunning and unafraid. Man was beginning his rapid conquest of the world.

True to their nature the dragons retreated. In some areas they were destroyed, but in remoter fastnesses they managed to survive. Mature males were not, in fact, very vulnerable to attacks by man in those early stages of the Stone Age. Clubs and traps were no use against them, and in any case they laired in places which were not of much interest to the new ape. The destruction of dragon populations would have been achieved at the breeding-pools, and where the females and young had inhabited the fertile plains the stock must have died out soonest. As soon as Man ceased to be a pure hunter, and needed the pools as drinking-places for his cattle or to provide water for his crops, the process accelerated, until there were huge areas of the world where no dragons flew any longer.

But elsewhere, along the fringes of the mountains and the deserts, a different sort of equilibrium might well have established itself. As man settled he planted, and where crops grew he became dependent on weather, and weather was dependent on who knows what? Something at any rate outside and beyond human understanding, but something at least which seemed at home in the sky. A flying god. Wherever dragons are associated with the gods, their chief concern

---

Cracus, who later named the city of Cracow after himself, slew an immense Dragon which laired in the aforementioned crag. For this devouring monster would issue from its cave and slay many people with its virulent breath, as foul as any plague. And wandering through the state and the region about it, it would devour whomsoever it met. Wherefore the inhabitants, to avoid this unpleasantness, decided to offer the beast at the mouth of its cave three cattle every day. Then Cracus, taking pity on the unhappy lot of his subjects, gave orders that the hide of a fresh-killed heifer should be stuffed with nitre and tar and sulphur and substances of that nature and placed by the mouth of the cavern. Whereon the hungry monster, creeping forth and thinking it to be a real heifer, swallowed the hide. Then the substances, especially the sulphur, caught fire within, and raised such a thirst that the animal charged out of its cave and hastened to the Vistula, where it drank so much water that its stomach burst and it died.

Ulysses Aldrovandus Historia Serpentium et Draconum

80

The standard explanation for the dragon/princess/hero legends is that they are an aspect of the age-old conflict between the human sexes. Parallel imagery can be seen either in the form of religious myth – e.g. the goddess Tiamat in the Babylonian creation myth, or the legend of the Sphinx or Medusa (p 104); or else it can be considered along Freudian lines as erotic symbolism *(left)*. The latter argument proves nothing – is, if anything, evidence for the existence of real dragons. On the whole, Freudian imagery transfigures but does not create. The creatures of our dreams are versions of the actual world.

As for the Sphinx and Medusa, they could well be a typically Greek effort to envisage a legend, distorted through innumerable tellings, in concrete terms. Certain elements would remain as essential – a large body armed with formidable talons, wings, a face which once looked at could not be turned away from. The concrete-minded Greeks would express these in known terms – body of a lion, wings of an eagle, face of a fascinating woman. But their tendency to refine ideas might also reduce the image to its central power, the eye whose stare can turn a man to stone.

is with rain and clouds and thunder — that is only natural even if dragons are purely mythical creatures.

But how much more natural it is if they were real.

Men needed gods, to protect their crops. They were even prepared to make elaborate sacrifices to them — usually an animal, but on special festivals or in times of drought a human, a young girl decked with flowers and jewels. In such societies daughters are often a surplus commodity. The story might have been different if it had been young males who were required — and not only from the point of view of those young males. The dragon would not have welcomed a prey which was likely to fight back. Indeed, he might well refuse it, to the worshippers' terror, so the tradition would grow up that the chosen victim must go calmly and nobly to her doom, must act in fact like a princess, and never dream of kicking and scratching — as a peasant girl might be sensible enough to do. Hence the persistence of princesses in all the stories.

So, with all his needs supplied by his worshippers, the dragon would no longer need to raid, to swoop out of the dark, burning the thatched huts, driving the defenders away so that it could snatch its prey in safety.

An arrangement like this might become entirely stable and last through many generations of men and dragons. The villagers might not much distinguish between the old dragon and the new one which took the lair over. The dragon would of course be largely a parasite, though the rumour of its presence might provide some protection for the worshippers against human enemies. At any rate the combination of custom and reverence and dread and difficulty would be quite enough to prevent them doing anything to remove it, and when they forgot their duty the dragon would become hungry enough to risk raiding again; the villagers would recognise the wrath of the god, and the custom would re-build itself anew.

Then at last the deliverer came, the stranger with the sword.

History is not at all tidy. For our own convenience we divide it into periods and give them names — Stone Age, Middle Ages, Naughty Nineties and so on — and this makes it easy for us to forget that even now, in the Age of the Atom, there are still a few Stone Age communities surviving. While the Homeric warriors were smiting each other with their bronze swords round the walls of Troy, while Sisera was terrorising the Middle East with his nine hundred chariots of iron, there were still whole nations in which no one had thought of killing his brother with anything more lethal than a flint. Especially this would have been true on the fringes of civilisation, in the very places where the dragons still ruled.

The dragon is associated with Gods by all people . . . Close relation exists between the dragon myth and the cult of the Mother Goddess; this relationship explains the persistence of stories of human sacrifice, concern with thunder and cloud, and with treasure. It explains too the virtue of slaying the dragon, i.e. the slayer is protecting mankind from the malignancy of the god.

Larousse Encyclopedia of Mythology

There the man with a sword would have been as much at an advantage as the man with the musket was when Pizarro conquered the Incas, or the man with the Gatling when the Mahdi's supposedly invulnerable horde rushed screaming to its own slaughter at Omdurman.

So the stranger came to the frontier, looking for trouble.

The story, by the time it became legend, goes like this: A wandering knight comes to a city and finds its towers hung with black, its bells tolling and its people huddled inside the walls. The very landscape seems in mourning, for the dragon has been out burning field and farm, demanding his due. Lots have been drawn for the girl who is to be sacrificed, and this time it is the King's daughter. The gates of the city open, and with dragging steps and wailing music the black procession winds across the black plain. Only one figure in all that scene wears white — the princess, pale, huge-eyed with weeping, going to her death in her bridal dress. They take her to the fatal tree and bind her there with a gold chain, then retire to the city. Now the knight comes to the tree and offers to release the princess, but she begs him to leave her, because her death alone can save her people. He says he will fight the dragon. She tells him how many brave knights have died before, trying to do that. He is not deterred, but hides until the dragon comes. As it approaches the tree he rushes out and attacks it with his magical sword (which he has somehow acquired earlier in the story) and at one blow it becomes quite tame. The princess binds it with her girdle and they lead it to the city where amid scenes of wild rejoicing the knight smites off its head. It expires with a vile stink. Wagons are sent to its cave and bring back mountains of treasure. The knight marries the princess and becomes king when her father dies.

Africa produces elephants, but it is India that produces the largest, as well as the dragon, who is perpetually at war with the elephants.

Pliny Natural History

Then Achilles made at him, filled with an animal's fierceness . . .
His right hand hefted his spear. The spear-point glittered like starlight
As he planned his attack on Hector, scanning the muscular body
For the right place to strike. The limbs and torso were covered
By the good bronze armour which Hector had stripped from Patroclus
But just where the collar-bone reaches the neck, flesh showed.
So as Hector rushed in with his sword swinging upward, Achilles
Drove with his spear at that place, and the bronze point skewered the muscle
Clean through the neck.

Homer Iliad

We know this story as the Legend of St. George and the Dragon, but it is known under different names in every country in the world where there is any dragon-lore at all. Many of the details are the same, and those that differ can usually be seen to have been tacked on in order to fit the story into the later culture of that country. Orthodox scholarship puts this similarity down to the stories having all a single source, in ancient Babylon. They say the Babylonians assembled the myth from Egyptian elements and it just spread by diffusion. But

The mythic hero, or Protogeorge, is a recreation by later times of the image of an original dragon-slayer, whose feat founded a first dynasty and with it a kingdom. As the conquered dragon had previously been worshipped as the all-powerful weather-god, it was usually important for the human rulers to assume as many as they could of the dragon's attributes. In Chinese myth the dragons actually became the ancestors of the kings; elsewhere the ancestor remained the hero who had slain the dragon, but his image was presented in a manner that emphasised the dragon qualities of the royal house.

Note, in this example, the recreation of the dragon's mask, or "helm of terror", in armour; the symbolic skulls of birds and humans echo the litter of bones around a lair. The detail of the knight's left leg is interesting: is this a subconscious transference by the artist of another dragon attribute to the hero? Or is it an actual reminiscence of a particular dragon-fighter who had lost a leg in a previous encounter (cf. Nelson's empty sleeve)? The horse's head echoes the dragon's, too.

Non-mythic elements are discernible. The curious lance may be a picture of an actual weapon, preserved as a sacred object through many generations. It would be much handier in close encounters than the traditional jousting lance, and its numerous spikes liable to cause larger and hence more disabling punctures to flight-cavities. Note the dragon's fully binocular vision, rare in reptiles but essential for hypnotic attack. There is a suggestion in the pose of knight and dragon that in the original encounter the technique of ambush from the flank was successfully employed.

there is another way of accounting for the similarities: if dragons were real, and if they established the relationship with Man which I have outlined, then the pattern of dragon-slaying would usually have been the same. Let us re-tell the story from that point of view and see how many of the details fall into place.

Below the mountains, along the edge of the cultivated land, lie a string of peaceful villages. There is a dragon in one mountain and the villagers worship it, give it a sheep or calf every new moon, and at the summer solstice a human sacrifice — a girl from a family which can spare one. They do not grudge it these gifts — other villages make similar sacrifices to far less tangible gods — and they say that the dragon brings good weather. One day a stranger comes, a strong man scarred with many fights and carrying a weapon the like of which they have not seen, no flint axe or hammer but a long thin blade of apparently magical strength and sharpness. The stranger learns about their dragon — or very likely he has heard about it already and has come to look for it, for reasons of his own. He offers to kill the creature. The villagers ask him to go away, saying that they are quite happy as they are, there are enough victims to spare and the one thing that matters is that the weather should stay fine for the crops. With his magical sword, though, the stranger persuades them to change their minds.

The villagers give in, secretly praying that their god will rid them of this troublesome interloper; and no doubt many times the god obliged, because the stranger made some mistake — tried to tackle the dragon inside its lair, or at a time when it had plenty of gas to fly with and breathe fire with, or else he was caught by its stare and attacked only the head. Such histories do not become legend, except that they contribute to the number of knights who have failed to slay the monster before the arrival of the hero.

Successful dragon-slayers had to be lucky, or skilled, or both. There were several recognised techniques (see below), but for the hero-story it was important that the stranger should kill the beast unaided. He had no wish to dilute his glory, and the power that would flow from it. He would wait for the season when the main sacrifice was due, signalled both by the turn of the seasons or by the dragon coming from his cave, hungry and angry with the growth of his new flight-cavity, and burning a field or two. The villagers choose their victim, deck her with a few jewels and many flowers and lead her to the place of sacrifice, playing as they go a special wailing music to draw the dragon from his lair, rather as a snake-charmer draws his serpents from their basket. Then they retire, but the stranger lies in ambush, and as the dragon comes to the altar he attacks it from the flank. He is unlikely to kill it, even with several blows, because the vital organs composed such a small part of the whole animal, but the first couple of slashes would both prevent it from flying and destroy its ability to breathe fire.

And the wild beasts of the islands shall cry in their desolate houses and dragons in their pleasant palaces.

Isaiah 13, 22

After that it was almost harmless, and might indeed have been led back to the village on a rope before being dispatched.

Next the stranger would follow the dragon's trail back to its lair. (Even if it had arrived by flying, the lair would not be too difficult to find, because the presence of a dragon so polluted the place.) If indeed there was a hoard there — as I propose to show later there might well have been — he would now be a rich man. But in any case he would be powerful, though his magical sword might well have been somewhat spoilt by the corrosion of the dragon's acids. Still, he had slain a god, and unless he was unlucky enough to have the crops fail that year he would be in a position to take the god's place. He would reinforce his status by marrying the daughters of local notables — perhaps even, if she was attractive enough, the girl he had used as bait — and become a petty king. Minstrels would gather to his court and to legitimise his rule they would compose hymns about his noble deed. His heirs would take care to see that the story was kept alive, for the same reason, but the story-tellers would tend to vary the details, keeping it up to date in dress and manners, until the whole thing became legend, waiting for the invention of writing so that it could be set down and studied by scholars, who would then be able to point out the obvious Babylonian elements.

(Jim Eckert has been transposed by magic into the body of a dragon.)

. . . there was a crackling of branches. A screen of bushes some twenty feet away parted to disgorge a man in full plate armour . . . seated on a large, somewhat clumsy looking white horse.

Jim, interested, sat up for a better look.

It was, as things turned out, not the best possible move. Immediately, the man on horseback saw him and the visor came down with a clang, the long lance seemed to leap into one steel-gauntleted hand, there came a flash of golden spurs, and the white horse broke into a heavy-hooved gallop, directly for Jim.

"A Neville-Smythe! A Neville-Smythe!" roared the man, muffledly, within his helmet.

Gordon R. Dickson The Dragon and the George

(*overleaf*) One of the rare images which give a reasonable idea of the actual size of a mature dragon. Artists have tended to play this aspect of the subject down for a number of reasons. First there is the convention of exaggeration, whereby the scale of the unknown marvel is increased to two or three times the known reality, so that giants (for instance) seem to run between ten and twenty feet tall. By these conventions a dragon might be described as being five or even ten times as big as an ox, but not the actual a hundred times. Then there is the artist's difficulty in plausibly portraying a creature of the real size once the knowledge that all that bulk was weightless has been lost. What legs or wings would carry it, what ground would it not sink into? Finally, there is the problem of showing human actors against an enemy of this scale, of making it conceivable that the midget knight on his mouse of a horse could overcome so huge an enemy. The hero needs to be drawn on heroic scale (see page 85), whereas the heroine, as here, is allowed to be dwarfed so that the hopelessness and pathos of her plight can be more touching.

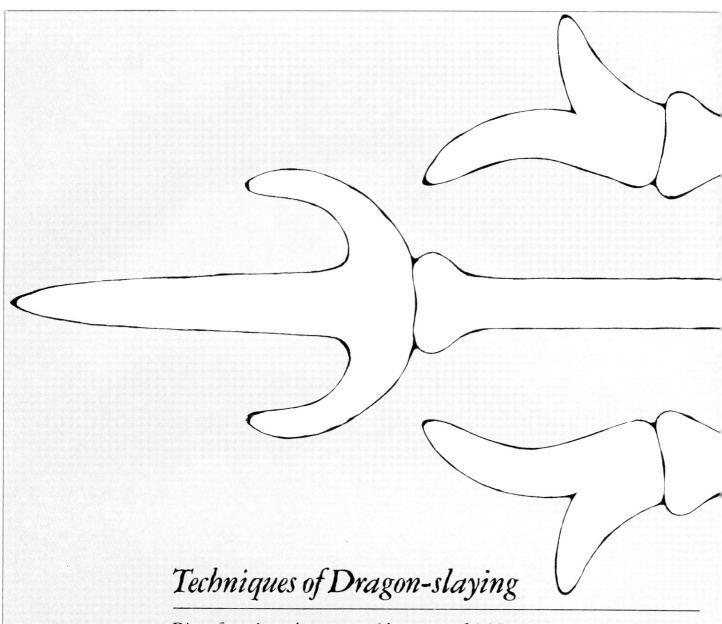

Techniques of Dragon-slaying

Direct frontal attack was very seldom successful. The commonest technique was ambush from the side when the dragon's normally sharp senses were concentrated on a victim. A variant, as in *Beowulf*, was for one man to lure the beast from its lair by seeming to attack it and then retreating, so that a colleague could slash it from the side as it emerged.

The attack from below was evidently a highly-developed skill. When earthbound because of immaturity or lack of gas, dragons would tend to follow well-worn trails because they would be in less danger of tearing their bodies. The attacker would find such a trail and dig a special series of pits in it and cover them with branches. The vital thing was that when the monster crept over him, the attacker should be able to smite it from below in such a way that any fluid spilt should not spray on him, but run off into a deeper pit. This was the method by which Sigurd slew Fafnir.

Various spiked traps evidently worked. More of More Hall killed the Dragon of Wantley by turning himself into a sort of bait and wearing spiked armour, and the Dragon of Corrie Lia, below Glencoe, was lured onto a spiked causeway

The Childe swore as the Wise Woman bid, and went his way to the smithy. There he had his armour studded with spear-heads, all over. Then he passed his vigils in Brugeford Chapel, and at dawn of day took his post on the Worm's Rock in the River Wear.

As dawn broke, the worm uncoiled its snaky twine from around the hill and came to its rock in the river. When it perceived the Childe waiting for it, it lashed the waters in its fury and wound its coils around the Childe, . . . but the more it pressed the deeper dug the spear-heads into its sides. . . . till all the water around was crimsoned with its blood. Then the Worm unwound itself and left the Childe free to use his sword. He raised it, brought it down, and cut the Worm in two.

The Lambton Worm retold by Joseph Jacobs

which was then set adrift. The Dragon of the North was evidently killed by some such means, but in many re-tellings of the story the original function of the iron spikes has been misinterpreted.

Finally, there is an interesting series of slayings by chemical means. In the Bible, in the Apocrypha book *Bel and the Dragon*, the prophet Daniel disposes of a dragon by giving it a lump of pitch, fat and hair to eat. The dragon swallows the bait and "bursts apart". Again we have a story in which a crucial detail has obviously been left out because of lack of comprehension by some copyist. The point about pitch and fat is that they burn fiercely. The hair was simply to bind them together. A dragon which could be induced to swallow such a gobbet would literally explode. The same technique was used to dispose of the Maister Stour Worm in the Orkneys.

Then Daniel said . . . But give me leave, O King, and I shall slay this dragon without sword or staff. And the king said, I give thee leave.

Then Daniel took pitch, and fat, and hair, and did seethe them together, and made lumps thereof: this he put in the dragon's mouth, and the dragon burst in sunder.

Bel and the Dragon

The old man said: "You are following the advice of one who wishes you evil. Reginn would have you kill the dragon — but perish in the battle so that he can take all the treasure. What you should do is dig a deep pit with a shallow trench running out from the side of it, so that you may lie in the trench while the dragon's blood falls only into the pit after you have stabbed him to the heart with the good sword Gram."

Having said this, the old man vanished, and Sigurd realised that it had been none other than Odin, King of the Gods of Asgard, who had spoken to him.

Sigurd the Dragon-slayer retold by Roger Lancelyn Green

THE DRAGON HOARD

"There he lay, a vast red-gold dragon, fast asleep . . . Beneath him, under all his limbs and his huge coiled tail, and about him on all sides stretching away across the unseen floors, lay countless piles of precious things, gold wrought and unwrought, gems and jewels, and silver red-stained in the ruddy light."

J. R. R. Tolkien *The Hobbit*

There are two major pieces of dragon-lore which I have so far left unexplained, because both arose from the dragon's contact with Man. They are the hoarding of gold and the ability to converse with humans. Though I believe that gold-hoarding took place and that genuine speech did not, I find the gold-hoarding harder to account for.

First, we must clear away the idea that dragons hoarded gold because it was valuable — valuable in the human sense, that is. Either they had a genuine need for it, or the habit was what naturalists call a displacement activity — something an animal does because it is prevented from doing what its main urge has been driving it to do. For instance, if I am angry with you I may have the urge to smite you. My arm begins to move to that end. But convention, or the presence of a policeman, prevents me from the actual deed, and so the arm finds itself raising the hand to scratch the back of my head which was not in fact itching. Or a gull, prevented from mating, may make rudimentary efforts to start building a nest, even in a hopeless place at the wrong season. And so on. I think it possible that a displacement activity and a genuine need reinforced each other to build up in dragons the extraordinary habit which I prefer to call gold-nesting.

Whenever the Dragon Prince does anything marvellous, the king comes and beseeches him, using gold, precious stones, pearls and valuables.

The Yuan Kien Lei Han

Apart from its value to man gold has two relevant qualities: it is one of the softest of all metals and it is chemically inert. Of course it is not soft in the way a feather mattress is soft, but it is incapable of forming points and edges sharp enough to tear a dragon's hide. Its inertness has two important effects: first, it is commonly found in its pure state as nuggets which could be collected even before the arrival of another gold-seeker, man, on the scene; and second, it was not affected by the ferocious juices that continually oozed from the dragon's body.

This last is the most important point. Wherever a dragon habitually lay would rapidly become a chemical quagmire, and dragons were forced by their life cycle to lie in the same place over long periods. Furthermore, as one of the essential processes in a dragon's survival was the minimising of weight, it could not afford to lie long in a quagmire, because its body would then tend to be coated with sludge, and a coat of sludge that size would weigh far more than a dragon could afford. Lengthy cleansing would be necessary before each flight (a fact which helps to account for the tendency of dragons to prefer to crawl on short journeys, rather than fly.)

So a gold-nest would be an ideal resting-place for a dragon. The metal would be safe and tolerably comfortable for an almost weightless body to lie on, and the chemical juices would drain down between the nuggets and other objects without forming sludge and without destroying the nest. That much is clear. We can account for the habit once it is fully established. The problem, as with so many other of nature's marvels, is to account for it having evolved in the first place.

I think the full development of the habit must be left to the era of the contact with man, and man in a fairly high state of civilisation. But we can lay a certain amount of groundwork before that era. For the reasons outlined above, even before the availability of gold some kind of nesting would be essential, a lair of fairly inert smooth boulders which would have to be replaced as the acids gradually destroyed them. Lairs being passed on from generation to generation, the most suitable materials would tend to survive longest, and come to be recognised by instinct as the proper stuff to build nests of. There might even by a few nuggets among the mess.

Then there is an aspect of dragon metabolism which I have only briefly referred to. In order to produce enough calcium for the main chemical reaction they would have to digest limestone, but it is unlikely that their jaws were very well suited for grinding up rocks. It is far more probable, in view of their parallel evolution with birds, that they relied on some sort of crop for this purpose. But whereas birds need only swallow small stones to grind up the seeds they eat,

---

Then Regin asked Fafnir to go shares in the gold, but Fafnir replied that there was little likelihood that he would share with his brother the gold for which he had killed his father, and he told Regin to go away or else he would meet with Hreidmar's fate . . . Regin took flight, but Fafnir went up onto Gnita heath and, making a lair there, turned himself into a dragon and lay down upon the gold.

The Prose Edda

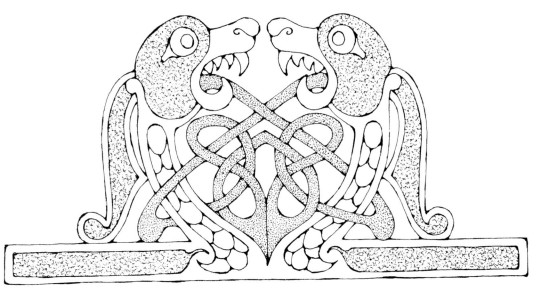

dragons needed something hard enough to grind up limestone. Very few natural materials would be suitable, but among them would be gemstones — diamonds, rubies, and so on. Obviously such materials were never common, but it must be remembered that where a dragon died in its lair its successor almost certainly ate whatever remained of the body, and this would include the contents of the crop. In fact we have here another natural mechanism for limiting dragon populations. Until a young dragon has taken over a lair and consumed the crop of an old dragon, he is unlikely to be able to produce enough gas to fly.

We also have an explanation of why the natives — in the passage from Jordanus

---

As one, dragons swivelled their wedge-shaped heads to their riders for firestone. Great jaws macerated the hunks. The fragments were swallowed and more firestone was demanded. Inside the beasts, acids churned and the poisonous phosphines were readied. When the dragons belched forth gas, it would ignite in the air into ravening flame to sear the Threads from the sky.

Anne McCaffrey Dragonflight

(*overleaf*) It is difficult to guess what metabolic changes may have come over the mature male dragon after he had retired from competition for domination over a breeding-pool. It is possible that with no further reproductive function, nature would arrange for his rapid dissolution, speeded by the violent chemistry of his metabolism. This would free scarce lairing-caves for younger males, still active in the struggle to breed.

On the other hand there are hints in many reports from travellers that the dragons of the remoter mountain passes were — even by dragon standards – unusually morose, treacherous and old. They were also normally flightless. We must think, therefore, of ageing dragons retiring to such areas and finding fresh lairs. They would no longer need the specialisation of flight, but would compensate for its loss with tougher and heavier hides to cope with harsher conditions. They would not find it easy to accumulate a new hoard among the poverty-stricken mountain-tribes, and this would add to their frustrations. But no doubt they would spend much of their time in a state something like hibernation, dreaming their remote lizard dreams of jewels, and thermal-soaring, and fire-fights above the breeding-pools, and succulent white sacrifices.

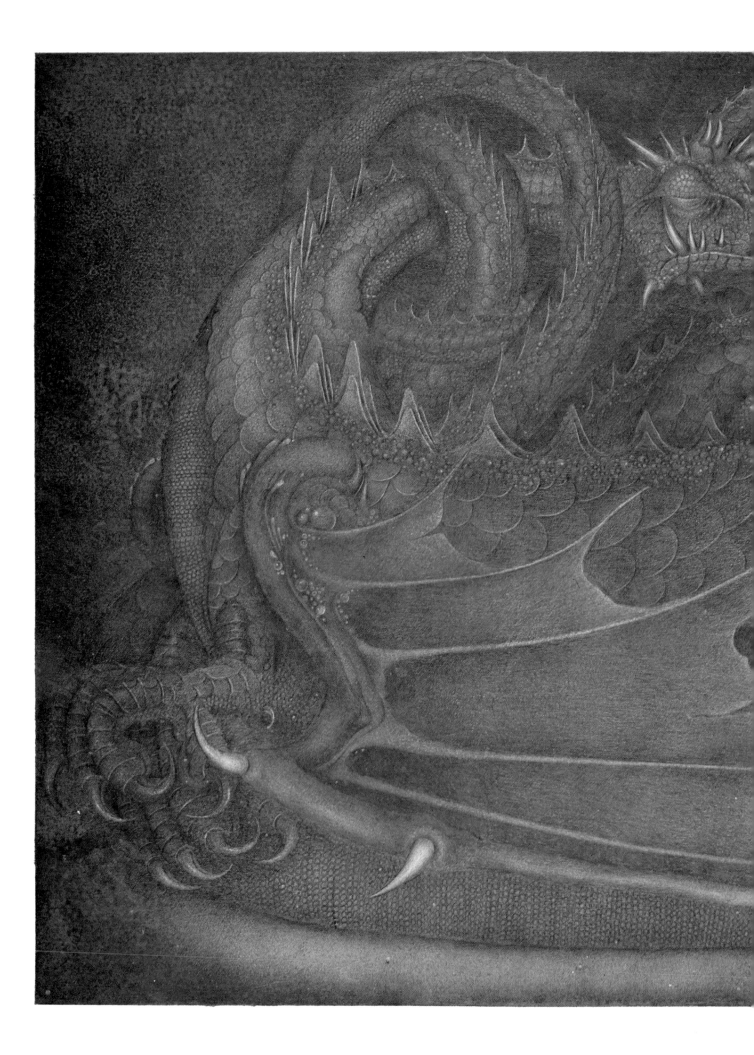

on page 27 — went to the place where a dragon had fallen expecting to find jewels there.

This brings me to the impact of man. One of the peculiarities of the human ape is the tendency to adorn the females, for ceremonial purposes, with gold and jewels. Few things are more ceremonial than a human sacrifice to a god. The dragon, in consuming its victim, might well find that it had been offered — as seasoning, so to speak — a few of the little hard things that were useful for grinding rocks up and some of that other stuff that was comfortable to lie on. It might not even recognise the gold, but if it took its meal back to the safety of its lair, it would naturally prize the gems from their settings and consume them. It would discard the gold, of course, not being able to afford the weight in its crop, and so the gold would join the material of the nest. Then, while the other nest material slowly decayed, the gold would remain and accumulate.

No one dragon would gather a whole hoard, all by itself. But as tenant followed tenant in the lair the nest would slowly become a dazzling mound, stretching from wall to wall, with its terrifying owner coiled on top. And at this stage I think that the hoarding habit would be reinforced by displacement-activity. In my outline of the life cycle of the dragon I have

---

The bottle . . . had swollen to three times its proper size, and seemed to be nearly red hot, and the air got warmer and warmer and the bottle bigger and bigger, till all the junior secretaries agreed that the place was too hot to hold them, and out they went, tumbling over each other in their haste, and just as the last got out and locked the door the bottle burst, and out came the dragon, very fiery, and swelling more and more every minute, and he began to eat the sacks of gold, and crunch up the pearls and diamonds and rubies as you do "hundreds and thousands".

E. Nesbit The Fiery Dragon

suggested that male dragons passed year after year without being able to mate, both before they achieved the status of bull-dragon and after they had been driven from that post. The long suppression of the sexual urge is bound to lead to strange behaviour, and to reinforce and exaggerate existing habits and urges. So it could well give rise to the notorious greed and rapacity of dragons, the tendency not only to accumulate gold and treasure as it became available, but to go out and hunt for it. Suppose the worshippers failed to appease their god with a jewel-decked virgin — suppose they tried to fob the beast off with garlands of marigold — then would come a night when the dragon's anger was roused enough to overcome its basic timidity, and it would come silently out on the night wind to search for what it needed, drifting down the dark, hovering over a sleeping settlement, and signalling its presence by a sudden blast of flame which would set a whole hut roaring. Who would then dare come out and face their god in his anger? Sometimes, no doubt, a defence was organised, and the dragon might even by driven off or killed. (Smaug's attack on Laketown is a vivid picture of such an incident, attributing though it does greater fire-breathing ability and more armour to the dragon than any real dragon is likely to have possessed.) But mostly the terrified villagers would carry their treasures to their doors and leave

---

"I . . .?" Gorbash grunted like a dragon just hit in the solar plexus by a particularly powerful ogre. "I? I've practically nothing, no hoard at all to speak of —"

"You lie!" cried Secoh. "You were next of kin to that great dragon, your grand-uncle. As next of kin, you've been told where his hoard lies; and since he was very old he was very rich from years of hoarding. You have two hoards, let alone one; and you're a wealthy dragon!"

Gordon R. Dickson The Dragon and the George

them on their thresholds. The dragon would take what he wanted and leave them in peace while he went back to coil himself up again on his great gold nest.

A question remains to be answered. Why have no hoards been found in later days? The answer must be that effective gold-nesting was only possible where dragons lived in this parasitic relationship with man, so when a dragon died, as soon as men became aware of the fact, somebody would be brave enough to go and look. Experts say that there was more gold in the ancient world than could be accounted for by known mining activities, and it is possible that the discovery and dispersal of dragon hoards accounts for some of it. But it is also possible that somewhere in the remote ranges there is a cavern, long blocked by a rockfall, where one day a modern caver may penetrate and find glittering under the beam of his lamp the heaped magnificence that was gathered there by the last of the great dragons.

They be strange creatures, these dragons. Over all the world 'tis the same with them: they gloat over treasure, and value it above all things else. In caves or burial mounds they gather great hoards: and should even the smallest of its jewels be stolen, a dragon would pursue the thief in deadly hate even unto the world's end. Yea, and a man might give it an hundred gold rings in exchange, but still it would know if its own ring was not among them . . .

Roger Lancelyn Green The Wonderful Stranger

(right) Once the gene for "gold-nesting" had evolved, there is no reason to suppose that further evolution would not take place. Many species – nearly all of them flying animals – carry similar behaviour to extremes which give them no imaginable advantage in evolutionary terms. Thus the original "gold-nesting" gene had every chance of being further adapted until it became a full-blown habit of treasure-hoarding. Then the choice of a cave would cease to depend solely on its suitability as a lair, and become a matter of its advantages for the hoarding, and even for the display, of treasure. In the unguessable mind of a dragon the hoard might eventually become curiously similar to what the art collection has become to many a human millionaire. The notorious lust for gold of dragons need not be a mythic extension of a not very marked behaviour pattern. It could be a report of actual fact.

Cave-paintings

As far as I know there are no cave-paintings of dragons. This may at first seem surprising, in view of the close and quasi-religious connection between man and dragon in the Stone Age. Two things account for it. The first is quite simple— in areas where dragons were cave-dwellers, men were not. The second depends on the function of cave-painting. It was a magical activity. The animals portrayed were those which the hunters wanted to encounter, kill and bring home, not only for food. For instance, the sabre-tooth must have been dangerous, but its fangs made heroic ornaments and its pelt was a chieftain's prize; and no doubt its flesh was edible, if chewy. But no hunter would wish to encounter a dragon, and there was no part of it which was the slightest use to anyone. To draw one, to invite it magically towards you, would be to invite horror and terror on your tribe. Even those who, like Hercules, attempted to harness its magical power came to a bad end by having done so.

DRAGON SPEECH

"The question is always the same with a dragon: will he talk with you or will he eat you? If you can count on his doing the former, and not doing the latter, why then you're a dragonlord."

Ursula LeGuin, *The Tombs of Atuan*

I have made very little use so far of Greek legend, though the Greeks told of several dragons. One guarded the Golden Fleece, another the golden apples of the Hesperides (both clearly hoarders). Another was killed by the hero Cadmus. And there were other monsters with strongly dragon characteristics, such as the Sphinx and Medusa. The word "dragon" itself is of Greek derivation, and seems to be connected with the verb for seeing. The Greeks thought of the dragons as lookers.

This brings me to two characteristic elements in almost all legends: you must not meet a dragon's gaze or you will be powerless; and the dragon will speak to you, in riddles, and will seem to know as much about you as you know yourself.

The Sphinx, for instance, was a flying monster which perched on the crags near Thebes and compelled all travellers to answer a riddle. Those that failed it

---

"Oh, it's pies, is it?" said Constantes. And he made as if to climb onto the big shovel, and tumbled off again. He did this several times. Then he said, "You'll have to show me how to do it, mistress dragon. I can't get the hang of it somehow."

Said the dragoness, "Why, young man, where's your wits? You get on like this."

She got up onto the shovel, and Constantes snatched the duster with the crown in it off her head, and gave her a push, and she slid off the shovel into the oven. And Constantes slammed the oven door and ran off with the ruby crown.

Constantes and the Dragon *Greek folk-tale re-told by Ruth Manning-Sanders*

threw down from the rocks and devoured. At last the hero Oedipus came by, and guessed the answer, and then it screamed and flew away. Note, for the moment that it flew, that it "compelled" an answer, and that the answer turned out to be Man — that is to say Oedipus himself.

The gorgon Medusa was a woman with snakes instead of hair. Her gaze could turn any living creature to stone, and she was eventually killed by Perseus who used a polished shield as a mirror to look at her indirectly when he attacked her. I don't think much can be made of the connection dragons/snakes/snake-hair. It is simpler to say that the Greeks were very human-centred in their view of this world and the world beyond. For instance, the original bull-god their ancestors had worshipped ceased to be a bull and became an aspect of Zeus, who sometimes turned himself into a bull for his own purposes. They thought in very concrete terms. Thus, in re-telling the tale of a hero who killed an apparently hypnotic opponent, they might well convert a monster which they could no longer satisfactorily envisage into a woman. I will explain the detail of the mirror-surfaced shield later.

Another famous legend from a different culture has a bearing here. This is the slaying of Fafnir by Sigurd. The story is told in a number of versions in most Scandinavian folklore, with many variants, but basically it goes like this. Fafnir and Regin are sons of Hreidmar. As a blood-price for the death of a third brother they are given a gold-hoard. Fafnir then kills his father, takes his father's "helm of terror" and the gold, and turns himself into a dragon to guard the hoard. Regin then forges a magical sword and tricks the young hero Sigurd into attempting to kill the dragon. Sigurd does this, by the pit-technique described on page 40. As he is dying, Fafnir asks who has killed him and why he was not afraid of the helm of terror. Sigurd refuses to reveal his identity, but Fafnir somehow knows it, and prophesies doom on the possessor of the hoard. Regin then asks Sigurd to cook the dragon's heart for him, and in doing so Sigurd accidently swallows a little of the blood from the heart. Immediately he can understand the language of birds, and thus learns from a pair of nuthatches that Regin is planning to kill him. He kills Regin and takes over the hoard.

This story of course contains almost all the major fragments of the dragon-myth, except flying and fire-breathing. (Presumably Fafnir is based on a large but as yet immature male.) The details that concern us here are first the helm of terror and second Fafnir's knowing who Sigurd is without being told.

The tiger looked leisurely for some ten seconds, and then deliberately lowered his head, his chin dropped and drawn in, staring intently at the man. . . . it was a piece of natural mesmerism that he had practised many times on his quarry, and though Chinn was by no means a terrified heifer, he stood for a while, held by the extraordinary oddity of the attack. The head — the body seemed to have been packed away behind it — crept nearer . . .

"My word!" he thought. "He's trying to frighten me!" and fired between the saucer-like eyes, leaping aside upon the shot.

Rudyard Kipling The Tomb of his Ancestors

The interesting thing about the helm of terror is that it plays no part whatever in the story, and many modern versions leave it out. The classic versions carefully explain about Hreidmar owning this precious object, though some of them have Fafnir wearing it when he kills his father. But in the earliest versions it simply crops up in the conversation between Fafnir and Sigurd, and is referred to several times, without any explanation whatever. So the business about Hreidmar having owned it seems to be a later tidying-up of the story by tellers who no longer realised that a helm of terror was a proper thing for dragons to possess. It was, in fact, what I have hitherto referred to as the dragon mask. It had two functions. It was a helm because it provided protection for the fragile dragon skull, and it was of terror because it was an essential element in the dragon's hypnotic armoury.

I have referred in earlier sections to the dragon's hypnotic powers, without explaining why I believe they existed or how they evolved as a necessary adjunct to the main specialisation of lighter-than-air flight. The time has now come to do so. I believe in the hypnotic powers because it is the only way in which I can account for the well-documented phenomenon of dragon speech. I cannot accept that dragons really spoke. Speech is a primary specialisation, and it is impossible that an animal already highly specialised in another direction should have evolved it, and evolved it in a form which permitted conversation in all the hundreds of human languages which must have existed, even in the Stone Age. Speech both demands intelligence and produces it. I am not saying that human intelligence is the only possible kind, but that it is impossible that dragons could

---

Ged stared in awe. There was no song or tale could prepare him for this sight. Almost he stared into the dragon's eyes and was caught, for one cannot look into a dragon's eyes. He glanced away from the oily green gaze.

Ursula Le Guin A Wizard of Earthsea

"I will give you seven years of freedom," said the dragon. "At the end of that time I will ask you a riddle. If you guess it the bargain is ended. But if you cannot guess it you must be my servants through all eternity."

Grimm The Dragon and his Grandmother

(overleaf) It is almost impossible to envisage or re-create in pictorial terms the physical reality of the dragon stare. Are we to take a hint from the frequent references to mirrors as a technique for defence against the stare that some form of light-reflection took place in the pupil of the huge eye? Or is it more likely that such stories are as near as oral tradition could come to conveying the sense of helpless self-awareness experienced by the victim? Modern research into the separate functions of the lobes of the brain suggests that the stare may have functioned by introducing an element of discontinuity into the victim's brain by supplying feed-back to one lobe out of phase to that supplied to the other lobe. If so, the concept of a magical mirror is as close as one can come to the actuality.

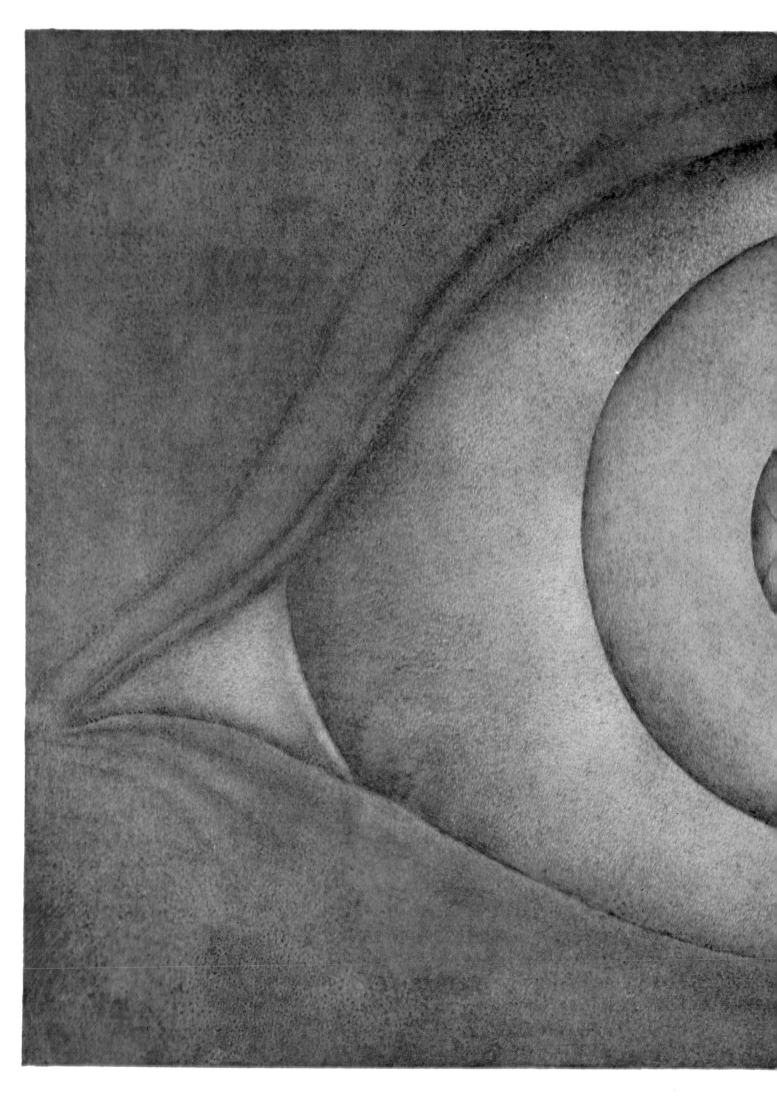

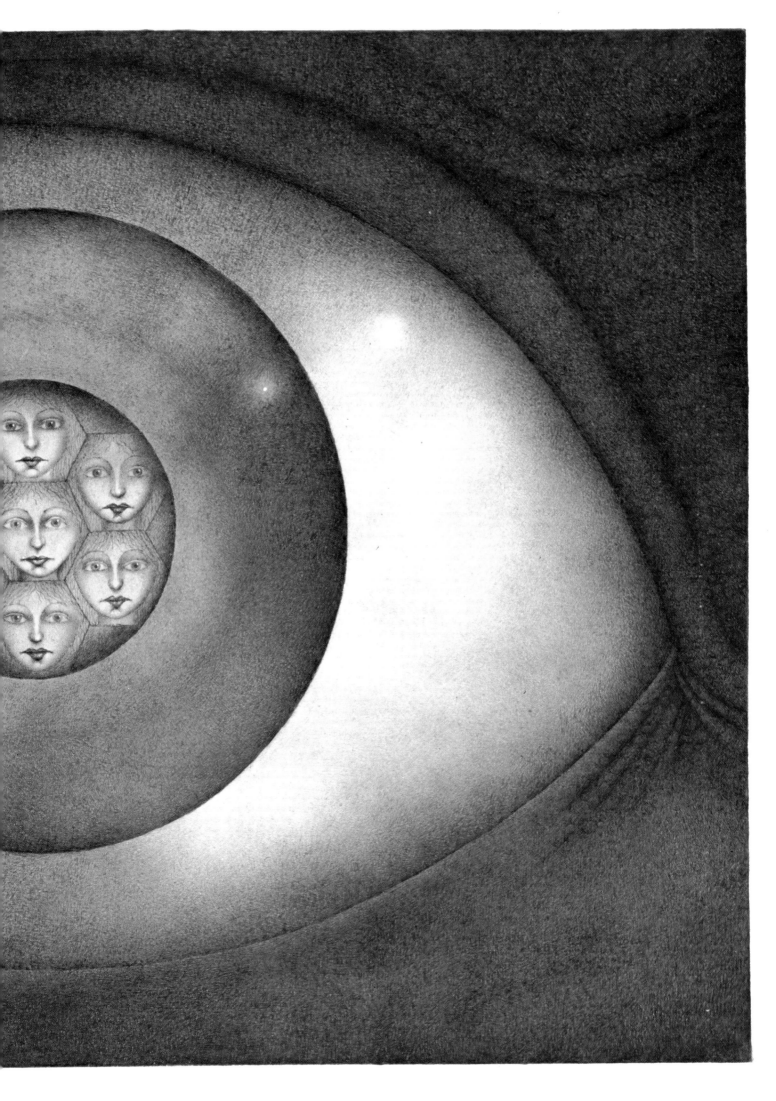

have evolved an intelligence human-like enough for speech. As a matter of fact I don't think they were very intelligent. There is a whole class of dragon-legends which are concerned not with heroes but with peasants, and in these the peasants invariably win by out-manoeuvring the dragons, who are represented as being powerful, tricky, magical and knowing, but very slow-witted indeed. My guess is that this is how they really seemed to the Stone Age men who encountered them.

So how did hypnotic power evolve? It depends on three existing factors, all arising from the main specialisation of flight. The dragon was vulnerable; it was slow-moving; and it appeared both huge and formidable. It needed to hunt and to defend itself, that is to say it needed a method of catching prey which didn't depend on chasing it, and it needed a method of self-protection which didn't depend on fighting.

Evolution tends to work, so to speak, with the grain. Given a natural advantage, evolution will exaggerate and refine it. In this case the advantage was an appearance that was already thoroughly formidable. An animal which is already to some extent protected by its ferocious aspect will tend to become more and more fearsome to look at, until any creature confronted by it is likely to be thrown into a trance of terror. From there to the power to induce hypnotic trance is not a long step.

Such hypnosis is not uncommon in nature. The best-known example is the ability of certain snakes to make their prey freeze where it stands and wait to be swallowed alive. Even Man is not wholly immune to this kind of attack. Tiger-hunters, in the great days of the Raj, sometimes found themselves half-trapped in the gaze of their intended victims; and if tigers, in whom the gift was not fully developed, could work the trick on Europeans armed with modern weapons and confident in the supremacy of their own scientific and materialist world-view, what must the effect of the gaze of a fully hypnotic dragon have been like upon Stone Age man?

It is not true to say we can have no idea, because shreds of the remembered experience remain buried in the stories. A stillness beyond terror, a sense of being asked a question whose answer is both obvious and impossible to find — the question which the Sphinx asked of the traveller and whose answer he could never see because it was himself.

Who am I? What am I? Why am I?

The questions would be wordless. There would only be a sense of asking. But when the trance was over the hero, like a man waking from a dream, would subconsciously re-shape its elements into things he could understand and explain. He would seem to have been looking at himself in a strange mirror. The self in that mirror would seem to have heard a language and grammar that was at once both familiar and incomprehensible, like a riddle. Both selves, several

---

This of course is the way to talk to dragons . . . no dragon can resist the fascination of riddling talk.

J. R. R. Tolkien The Hobbit

Four-legged at dawn,
Two-legged by day,
Three-legged at eve —
What creature, say?

selves, would have sought desperately for the answer, knowing that life depended on it. Then, if the hero had the resources of will and intelligence to draw these separate selves together he would find that between them they held the answer. He would break the trance and realise what was happening to him. Thus he would seem to himself to have answered the riddle.

He was Oedipus, he was man, he was there to slay the monster.

This accounts for the magical gaze of the dragon, and also for its apparently supernatural knowledge — what it appeared to know would in fact only be what the man himself knew, his name, his origins, things that nobody except himself could know. But once free of the dragon's gaze, through the barrier of terror, he would find his enemy no match for him either in intelligence or speed. It would seem slow-witted after all, easily tricked, easily slain.

I don't want to place too much emphasis on the business with the mirror. It is a device obvious enough for any story-teller needing to explain how a hero overcame the magical gaze of an enemy; but I think that its power as a symbol is stronger than that of a mere device. It seems to belong, in the way that true dragon-lore belongs, and this may be because it echoes an inner truth about dragon-encounters.

There is a final point about the mask, or helm of terror. When the growing dragon was in its lair, the head was the only place which could be attacked at all, so there was a natural tendency to evolve a head that would withstand attack — a light but corky mass of tissue over the thin bone beneath. This mask would evolve into shapes to aid the hypnotic effect, and there would also evolve a tendency for the hypnosis to concentrate the attack of any enemy — supposing an enemy was encountered which was not wholly mastered by the gaze — onto this one safe point. The truth is not that dragons had only one vulnerable spot, which the hero had to find, but that it had only one invulnerable spot, which the hero had to avoid. The fact that he failed so often is witness to the power of the dragon's eye.

BEOWULF

"Then spirted the serpent fearsome fire-brands,
Burning byre and barn and friendly farmstead.
Flared flames skyward in mock of mankind,
Nor would the wind-wanderer leave one life living."

Beowulf

Until I did the research for this book I had never tried to read *Beowulf*. I'd seen potted versions of it, which made it sound like a boring old story about a king who built a feasting-hall, and a hero who killed the monster that was raiding it, amid a good deal of boasting and disputes about etiquette. Now, thank heavens, I've found out that it is something quite different — though I've had to pick my way word by word through the Anglo-Saxon with a modern prose translation in my lap.

It turns out to be a magnificent strange poem about a professional dragon-killer and his fights with three separate dragons.

Scholars working on *Beowulf* tend to ignore the monsters, though anyone who reads the poem for the first time can see that they are of central importance. The scholars take them for granted, as fairy-tale intrusions, and concentrate on the picture of Anglo-Saxon life which the poem gives, and on things like the connection between its characters and real historical personages. Indeed, Oxford students who have to read the poem as part of their studies are supposed to stop two-thirds of the way through, and so miss out completely on the climax, the fight with the Fire-drake.

There may actually have been a man called Beowulf, but it's unlikely that he

*The glimmering gold was found and hoarded
By the horror of the half-light, the haunter of hills,
Scaly and spiteful, the dark-flying fire-drake.*

. . . they beheld the hand,
The fingers of the fiend, set up before them.
In the sockets the nails stood like new steel.
Spur-spiked was the hand of the heathen marauder
With terrible talons.

had the adventures narrated in the poem. Instead, he was a hero around whom certain kinds of folklore tended to gather, in much the same way that a lot of popular stories about thieving and outlawry got grouped into the Robin Hood legend, though Robin Hood also may or may not have been a real person.

The difference is that while the Robin Hood stories come down to us as a tangle of indifferent ballads, the Beowulf stories were re-shaped by a poet of great power. Consciously or unconsciously he knew what he was doing. He gave his story a shape, an architecture. Half that shape is the hero's own progress from dashing youth to age no less courageous but less foolhardy; and the balancing, or echoing half lies in the nature of the enemies he fought — first a young dragon, not yet fully mature but raiding on land by night; second, a mature female in her spawning-ground; and third, a mature male, flying and breathing fire.

This is why I am devoting a whole section to *Beowulf*. It is a remarkable example of how detailed and exact the folk-memory of dragons was all through the time it was being re-shaped through legend after legend, and how it remained so even when the legend-makers were no longer fully aware that the monsters they were describing were dragons.

The first monster is given a name, Grendel. He is barely described, but scholars have tended to assume that he was some sort of half-man, of huge size; he is said to be an outcast descended from Cain; he is only actually seen at third-hand — that is to say King Hrothgar tells Beowulf that some of his men have glimpsed him and that he walked man-fashion. The poet is deliberately vague about this, in a manner that adds to the horror and the mystery, but he allows us to see two details more closely: first, the monster's arm, which Beowulf tears from its socket while wrestling with him in the feasting-hall in the dark; and second, his head, which Beowulf cuts off and brings back as a trophy after killing both Grendel and his mother in her underwater lair. The arm, or rather

---

I have heard it spoken by subjects of mine
Who hold their halls up in the outlands
That they have seen there two such somethings —
Mighty march-stalkers haunting the moorlands,
Huge and inhuman. Yet one of them was
Of womanish sort, so far as they saw her.
One trod his ghastly tracks with the gait
Of a man, though monstrous beyond man's stature.

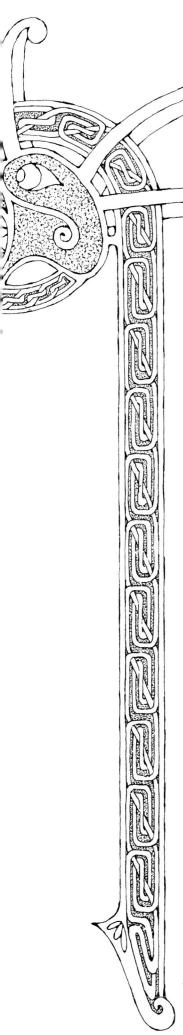

It was a great gauntlet,
Huge and hideous and belted with bindings,
A glove-thing geared in mysterious manner
With devilish skills and the skins of dragons.

the hand or "grip", is at first described merely as being of inhuman size and having impressive talons. But telling the story later Beowulf speaks as though he realised it was not a human hand at all, but something much more like a glove with peculiar machinery inside — just what we might expect to be left of a dragon-limb after the first rapid decay of the flesh, a covering of toughened hide, containing strange-shaped and lightweight bones. Beowulf actually says that the "glove" is made of dragon-skin. We are told less about the head, only that it is hideous and indescribable — clearly also not human.

We are told two other facts about Grendel. He leaves clear tracks across the moor; and when his head is cut off his blood so corrodes the blade of the sword that only the hilt is left. Other things can be deduced; he was certainly of inhuman size, because he could only raid into the feasting-hall, but was unable to molest people sleeping in ordinary huts. On his first raid he is said to have seized thirty sleeping warriors and carried them away, but that is clearly a poetic rather than a mathematical use of numbers. More interestingly, though a

---

To his hoard he hied him
To his dark dwelling before day's dawning.
He had fenced the farmers with his own flaming,
With bale and burning, but now he trusted
In his mountain walls and his wiles of warfare.
That trust betrayed him.

(overleaf) Grendel's Mother. A distinction has to be made between the fascinating monsters (Sphinx and Medusa) of Greek legend, and the hag-women and troll-women of the North. Only the latter are based on folk-memories of the female dragon; the former are attempts to account in concrete form for the effect of fascination, and are based on memories of the male's hypnotic gaze.

The female's hypnotic powers were weak or non-existent. She had no need to evolve such a weapon, as her body, not being weightless, was enormously tougher and she was protected for most of her life cycle by her aquatic mode of existence. This fact, together with her smaller size and biped gait when on land, accounts for the greater familiarity of man with her, and for the tendency for legend to make her more and more human, until she is often transmogrified into the cosy "Dragon's Grandmother" of folk-tale, who actually protects and defends the trespassing peasant-hero.

115

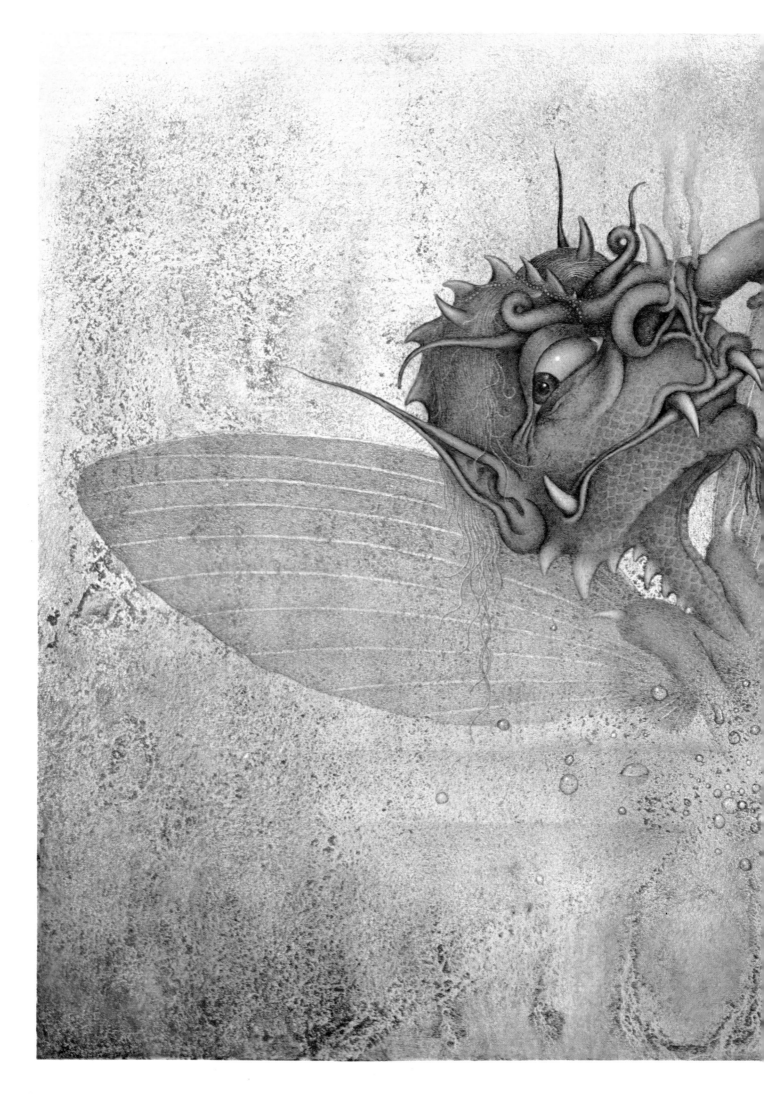

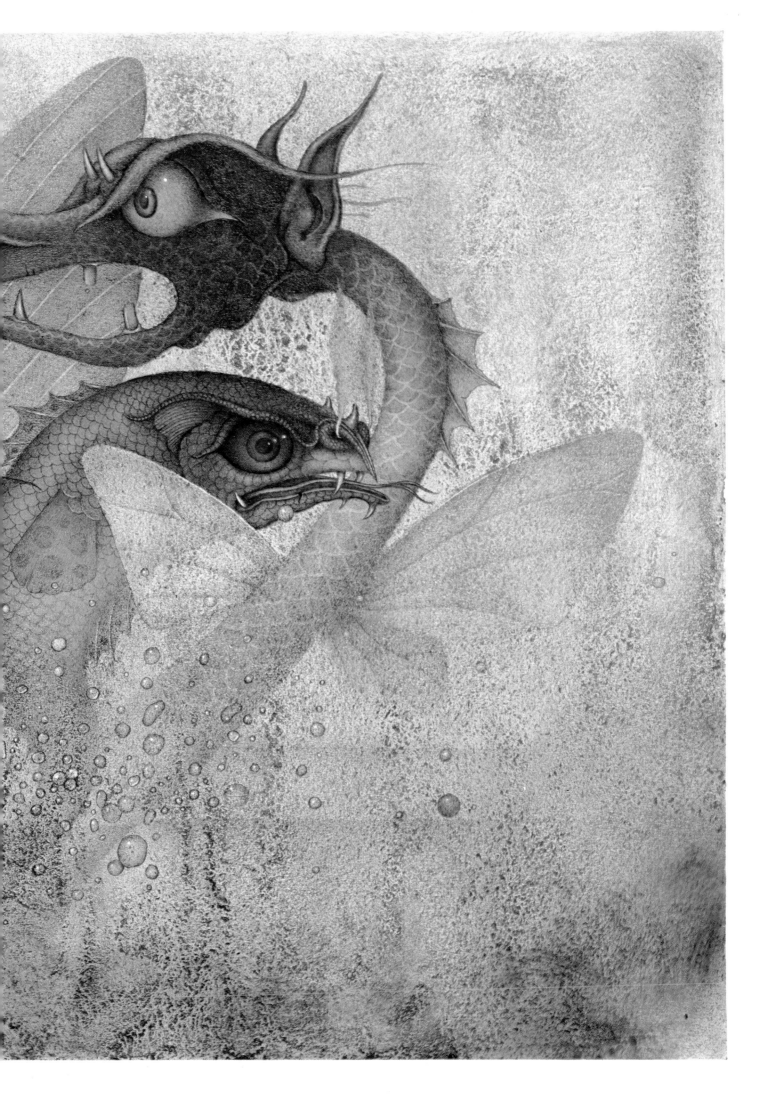

creature of great size he must be very fragile for Beowulf, however strong, to tear an arm from its socket.

(One can speculate upon the original event on which this part of the poem is based — a cave-dwelling people perhaps, who did not use a particular large cave because it tended to be visited by a marauding young dragon, but were happy to lodge strangers there as they satisfied the dragon's appetite. One of these strangers fought back and succeeded in killing the dragon by tearing its fore-limb out — that would be a feat sufficient to become legend.)

These details, though not enough in themselves to prove that Grendel was a young dragon, certainly point that way. Even the passage which appears to disprove it — Hrothgar's description of his men seeing Grendel and his mother, and their seeming human — fits in quite well. Dragons when not in danger did move man-fashion, on their hind legs, a trait inherited from their dinosaur ancestors. The event on which the next episode — the killing of Grendel's mother — is based concerns a female, and the original dragon-slayer presumably knew the difference. When the legends were welded together the story-tellers were probably still aware that they now had a male and a female monster; and when our poet came to create the final version he worked these elements in in a masterly way, creating an effect of half-seen horror which is increased by the hint that the monsters are somehow human and somehow not.

When we come to the episode with Grendel's mother we are on much surer ground — indeed, I can remember reading as a child an illustrated retelling of the Beowulf story in which the artist had drawn the mother as an out-and-out dragon. It must have seemed obvious to him, from the poem itself. In a way the most remarkable detail about this episode does not concern the mother, but the mere where she lives, a place of desolation, in and round which young monsters swim and bask. We have already been told that this is a place of danger — even the hunted deer will prefer to sell its life on the shore rather than try to swim that water. Beowulf shoots one of these water-beasts and his men harpoon it and drag it ashore. It is unlike anything they have ever seen. (Presumably the mere was large enough for several young, without the overcrowding that would have triggered the cannibalistic tendencies in more constricted waters.)

Beowulf had insisted on fighting Grendel unarmed, a point that has puzzled critics but can be explained by assuming that in the original legend the sleeping

---

Rowans hung over a hoary rock,
In a gloomy grove. Below it the water
Lay dull and troubled . . .
        The men beheld
How the mere was murky with warm blood-wellings.
They watched on the water many a worm-thing
Daunting sea-dragons diving and swimming,
While curious creatures lolled on the ledges
        . . . they slithered away,
Swollen with spite at the horn's bright blare.

warrior had not expected to be woken by a dragon. Now, however, he puts on his mail coat and takes a special sword and plunges into the water. He is at once attacked by the water-beasts, but Grendel's mother seizes him and drags him to her lair, which seems to be a cave with an underwater entrance. (Again, critics have been puzzled by Beowulf's finding himself suddenly able to breathe, despite being under water; but a cave of this sort would have been enormously valuable to a semi-aquatic but air-breathing creature such as the female dragon.) There is a weird phosphorescent light in the cave, as one would expect from a knowledge of the dragon metabolism. Beowulf attacks the monster with his sword, bringing it down on her head without harming her. He throws it away and wrestles with her, but she is too strong for him and draws a knife to finish him off. His armour saves him. Then he sees among her hoard an enormous old sword, forged by a giant, and with this he succeeds in striking her head off. He explores the cavern, finds Grendel dead or dying, and cuts his head off also. Grendel's blood causes the sword-blade to melt like ice in a thaw, leaving only the hilt. Beowulf takes this and Grendel's head as trophies and swims back to the surface.

Of course there are elements here that have to be explained in terms of the poet's own time. For instance the weapons involved have been updated, so that instead of a flint club and an iron sword they become two swords, one of which has to be quasi-magical to pierce the dragon's hide. Perhaps this then made it seem a little less than heroic for a hero with two swords to fight an unarmed female, so Grendel's mother is given a knife (which, even to the reader who doesn't support my theories, strikes a false note.)

It is interesting that though the female is smaller than the male, she too appears to have a well-protected head, and also the ability to concentrate attacks on it.

He looked no longer at the hideous head.
Burnt to the bone was the hand that had helped
In the fight for his friend, yet full strength he struck
Lower along the flank of the fire-drake.
So struck he. So slid the well-worked weapon
Right through the ribs. So of a sudden
Faded the flame.

The poet ties his first two legends together by making Grendel's mother raid King Hrothgar's hall in revenge for the wounding of her son; Beowulf then tracks her to the mere. This is of course a structural device to link episodes which originally involved quite different dragon-slayers, in different times and places. But the poet makes no attempt to provide a similar link to the third episode. He must have felt that the logic of progression was by then strong enough without it.

I don't have to prove that Beowulf's third adversary was a dragon, because the

poet says so — it flew, it breathed fire, it hoarded gold, it laired in a cave and its blood was poisonous. But for the sake of completeness I will finish the story, pointing out where it affects my theories.

Beowulf is now King of his own country, old and respected. One of his vassals finds a dragon-hoard and steals a cup from it. When the dragon discovers the loss he becomes enraged and begins to ravage the country. Beowulf has a special iron

---

. . . that wide wound
Which the dragon had dealt him, the old earth-dweller,
Blistered and bubbled. And soon he sensed
How the vile venom was working inwards.

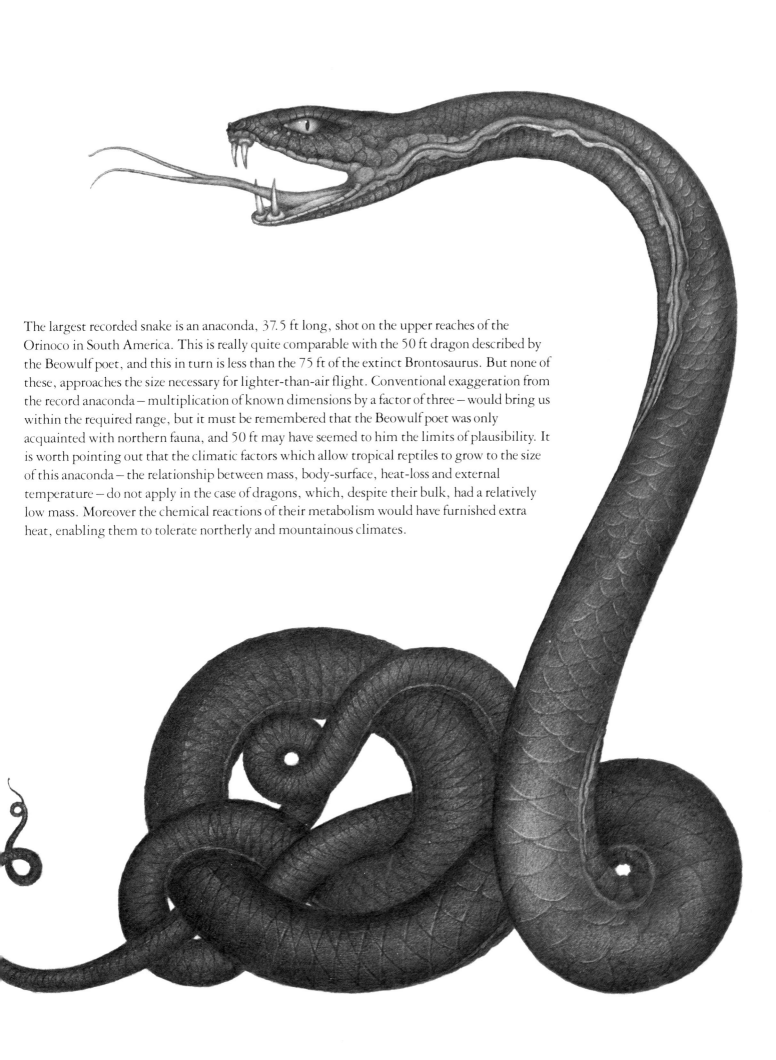

The largest recorded snake is an anaconda, 37.5 ft long, shot on the upper reaches of the Orinoco in South America. This is really quite comparable with the 50 ft dragon described by the Beowulf poet, and this in turn is less than the 75 ft of the extinct Brontosaurus. But none of these, approaches the size necessary for lighter-than-air flight. Conventional exaggeration from the record anaconda – multiplication of known dimensions by a factor of three – would bring us within the required range, but it must be remembered that the Beowulf poet was only acquainted with northern fauna, and 50 ft may have seemed to him the limits of plausibility. It is worth pointing out that the climatic factors which allow tropical reptiles to grow to the size of this anaconda – the relationship between mass, body-surface, heat-loss and external temperature – do not apply in the case of dragons, which, despite their bulk, had a relatively low mass. Moreover the chemical reactions of their metabolism would have furnished extra heat, enabling them to tolerate northerly and mountainous climates.

shield made and goes out to fight the monster. His men go with him, but do not help in the fight. At the lair Beowulf raises his war-shout and the dragon comes out, breathing fire. Beowulf strikes at its head, but without success and, despite his shield, is badly burnt. One of his men, Wiglaf, comes to help. His own wooden shield is burnt and he takes refuge behind Beowulf's. The fight is resumed, and now Beowulf's sword breaks in his hand and the dragon bites him in the neck, but at the same time Wiglaf strikes the animal "lower down" and pierces its hide. Immediately the fire slackens. Beowulf draws his hunting-knife and attacks the dragon "in the middle", and thus between them they kill it, apparently without further difficulty. Now Beowulf feels the poison from the dragon's bite eating into his body. Wiglaf brings out some of the hoard to show him before he dies.

I think what we have here is an account of one of the recognised dragon-slaying techniques which went wrong. Critics have been puzzled by Beowulf's insistence on fighting the dragon alone, though Wiglaf later upbraids his comrades for not helping their king when he is in mortal danger. In fact it would have been useless for a whole crowd of warriors to turn up at a dragon's lair — the creature would never have come out. It had to be baited out, by a man wearing and carrying special protective armour. It could then be attacked from the side, before it was sufficiently clear of its cave to fly. Hence the iron shield and the war-shout. But evidently the dragon on which this story is based spotted its second attacker and breathed fire at him, forcing him to take refuge with the first attacker, who was thus exposed to a second onslaught of flame. The first man seems to have been caught by the dragon gaze, and to have concentrated his attacks on the mask without success. But the second man seized his chance when the dragon was savaging the first man and returned to the original plan, striking at the vulnerable flight-cavities, so that the dragon could no longer breathe fire, and became an easy victim.

The poet says that the dragon's body was fifty feet long, which is a rare example of poetic understatement. It must have been at least twice that if the dragon was a mature flier. Perhaps he felt his audience might not believe him. He also says that the body was scorched with the beast's own flames, which is unlikely to be true; but it would certainly have begun to char with its own internal acids, released from the wounds in its flanks.

There is a facet of the whole poem which is difficult to summarise, or even to translate into modern English. When the poet describes the monsters,

---

Then viewed the victor
The gleam of gold-work, brooches and bracelets
Gravelling the ground, wonders on the walls
Of the dragon's den, the old dawn-flier,
And urns upright, once held by heroes
In elder ages, now all unburnished
With fretwork fallen, and helm and hauberk
Rotten with rust . . .

particularly the Fire-drake, he does so in a tone of violent disgust and anger. Sometimes he adopts Christian terms — Grendel and his mother are of the brood of Cain, enemies of God, outcasts for ever — but mostly the feeling is raw. The dragon is loathsome, grisly, monstrous. For the poet and his audience it is no kind of whimsy or fantasy. In those warriors who sat round the meadhall, listening to the bard in the vague lights and shadows from the central fire, it woke echoes of an ancient horror, a horror that had once been real.

(Note for pedants: the translations from Beowulf are my own, and I am well aware that Anglo-Saxon alliterative verse is not as alliterative as that. I have deliberately overdone it, because in short snatches the less aggressive alliteration of the long poem would be barely noticeable.)

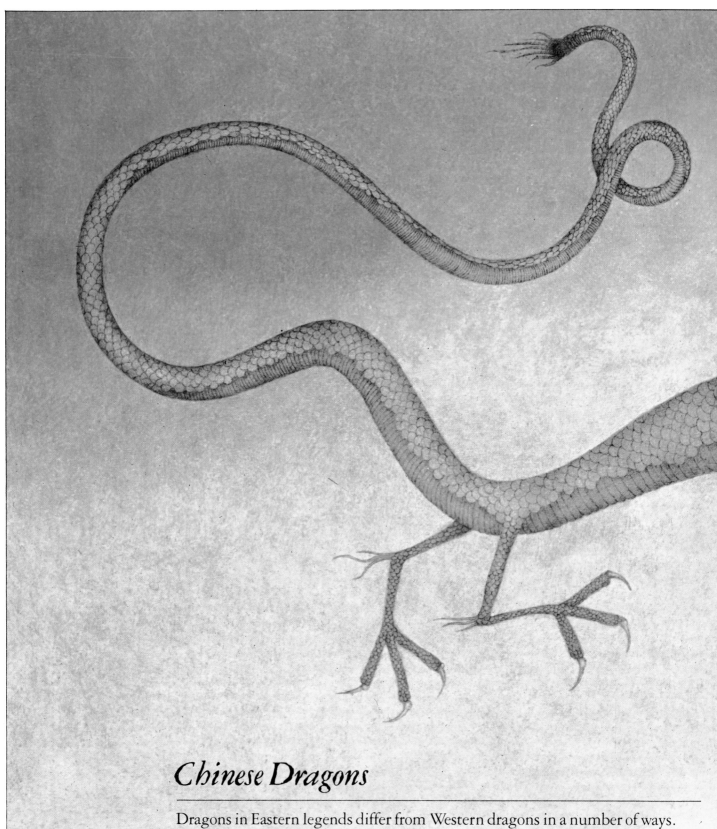

Chinese Dragons

Dragons in Eastern legends differ from Western dragons in a number of ways.
The most important are that they seldom breathe fire and they are benevolent, if
hot-tempered. Sometimes they are said to be wingless. The fact that Chinese art
depicts them by rather different stylisations tends to conceal a lot of similarities.
In China too they are seen as very large flying serpents. Their blood is magical.
They are associated both with mountains and with pools. They speak. It is
dangerous to look directly at them. And they hoard treasure.

If we assume, as seems likely, that the last stronghold of the dragons was up in the great Asian plateau, then it would not be surprising if the traditions that carried the stories east differed in detail from those that carried it west. The chief variations can be explained by the very early adoption by Chinese kings of the dragon as a sacred ancestor, a symbol of kingly power. That would put paid to the survival of legends of dragon-slaying (cult-heroes are not so tactless as to kill the

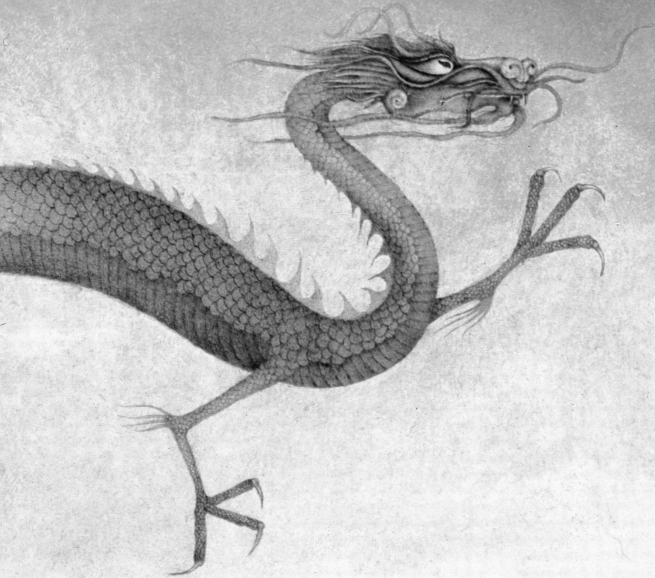

king's ancestors), and would thus minimise the emphasis on the dragon's chief weapon of terror, its fiery breath.

I think that in some ways the Chinese tradition of dragon portrayal may be closer to the truth than the western one. The mask is much more pronounced and hypnotic, the wings are less noticeable, and the body is more tubular and less tapering. Sometimes the body is drawn as a series of connected bulges, which may distantly echo the genuine external appearance of a body composed mainly of flight-cavities. It is noteworthy that Chinese dragons were able to alter their size.

EVIDENCE FOR DRAGONS

"Sometimes we see a cloud that's dragonish."

Shakespeare *Antony and Cleopatra*

As man came, the dragons went. Brief though the contact was, compared to the enormous spans of time in which species mature and flourish and die out, they have left their mark on us. Though their metabolic processes made it unlikely that an interpretable fossil bone of a dragon will ever be found, fossils of another kind are common enough. They are embedded in our minds, just as recognisable, once you know what to look for, as a real bone sticking out of a rock layer.

In a recent book, *The Dragons of Eden*, Professor Carl Sagan tried to account for the spread and consistency of dragon legends by saying that they are fossil memories of the time of the dinosaurs, come down to us through a general mammalian memory inherited from the early mammals, our ancestors, who had to compete with the great predatory lizards. This stretches the idea of fossil memory much further than I propose to, but the fact that it can be seriously suggested at all is significant.

A lot of our thought and behaviour is governed by fossil memory, though we seldom notice it. For instance, when we wake from a nightmare we tend to lie in the dark for a while with every muscle locked rigid. It takes a huge effort of will to twitch the first finger and begin to break the spell of terror. This reaction must surely trace back to an age when man was hunted as often as he was the hunter, and the reaction of total stillness at certain moments of peril was so necessary for his survival that it became an inherited instinct. Other memories stick out of our minds with no traceable origin. For instance, why do small children shudder with horror when they find a bit of red jelly in a crack of the cold chicken they are eating? What ancestral danger does that harmless blob evoke? And so on.

In the argument about dragons such fossil memories are more than a simple piece of general evidence. If all they did was provide a ghostly image of great flying lizards they would not be much use as witnesses. It is the detail that matters— the way in which they tell us what is right about a portrayal of a dragon and what is wrong. When we read in a work of fiction about an imaginary dragon we accept the writer's ideas with a strangely vehement certainty, or else we reject them irritably as wrong. We feel we know.

I have already pointed out how children will often draw a dragon wing more correctly than a trained artist because their fossil memories are not cluttered with the anatomy lessons of the art schools; but despite that the imagination of the artist is the best evidence we have. The way in which imaginative art works is as interesting, in its own fashion, as the anatomy of dragons. Writers and artists do not build even their most fanciful structures out of nothing. They take elements from the world outside them and elements from the other world within them, and by combining these they produce a chemistry in which something apparently new is created; and yet when we see or read that creation we have a sense of recognition, of rightness, about it, however strange it may be in its final form. This can only mean that the same elements the artist has used are also available to us, inside us and around us. All we lack is his chemistry. But we know them, subconsciously, even in their altered forms. Of course not all the inner elements we recognise consist of fossil memories, but I think more do than we generally realise.

Most accounts of dragons occur in works which are close to the springs of imaginative creation. That is to say they occur either in "primitive" legend, or else in books written for children. It doesn't matter to me that both these sorts of writing are the work of comparatively unsophisticated artists, in fact it is a positive advantage. Such artists have no aesthetic axes to grind, no deliberate theory about the nature of their art, no urge to break the pattern of previous

The Devil, in Christianised art, became *the* dragon. We are so used to the identification that it is hard for us to see that it is not a very logical piece of symbolism, if everybody really knew in their hearts that dragons were mythic monsters. Elsewhere Christian symbols are very concrete, following the traditions of the parables of Christ. The souls of men are sheep; the Holy Ghost is a dove; sinners are goats; the enemies of the Church are wolves, and so on. But if in men's subconscious memories dragons were real, and if on top of that they carried with them a deep implanted sense of horror and dread, then the image fits the reality.

Some Classic Variations

Opposite page:
1) *Top left:* Dragon, *Sevoro Calzetta, 16th Century*
2) *Centre left:* St. George and the Dragon, *Paolo Uccello, c.1460*
3) *Right:* St. George and the Dragon, *Gustave Moreau, 1890*
4) *Bottom:* Two Followers of Cadmus Devoured by a Dragon, *Cornelis van Haarlem, 1585*

This page:
5) *Left:* Altarpiece of St. George, *attributed to Marsal des Sas, 1236*
6) *Above:* Chest of Drawers, *Chinese 15th Century*

1, 5, 6: Victoria and Albert Museum, Crown Copyright
2, 3, 4: Courtesy of The National Gallery

art-forms. They are doing the oldest trick in the world — telling a story — and the details they put in are whatever seems to them right for the story. If they're on form their audience recognises that rightness.

So most of the evidence in this book comes from sources which wouldn't normally be considered evidence at all. No single quotation carries much weight, but taken all together they build up a remarkably consistent picture, not only where they agree with each other, but also in the odd detail which nobody else has thought of but which still fits in.

No doubt I have missed out a lot of useful material in my research, and readers who are interested are sure to be aware of other examples of dragon-lore, or to come across them in the future. They may care to see how well this fresh material fits into my theory, looking always for that telling combination of strangeness and rightness which is evidence of something stronger and older than a story-teller's whimsy.

Remember. The dragons live. Inside us.

Peter Dickinson was born in 1927 in the middle of Africa, within earshot of the Victoria Falls, but has lived most of his life in England. He won a scholarship to Eton, and enjoyed a very old-fashioned education there and at Cambridge, broken by an undistinguished spell in the army. For seventeen years he was an assistant editor at Punch.

His first books were published in 1968, and since then he has written about twenty, half of them slightly weird detective stories, and the remainder mostly children's adventure fantasies. Both kinds of work have won prizes, and have been published in ten languages.

He is married, has two adult daughters and two teenage sons. He spends half his time in a small house in West London, and the other half in a decayed Victorian dower house in Hampshire. He likes to do things for himself, from plumbing to thinking.

Wayne Anderson was born in England in 1946. He left school when he was 15 and went to Leicester College of Art where he spent 4 years studying graphic design. He then went to London and spent 5 years working there freelance.

He now lives in a Leicestershire village with his wife and their three children; two daughters and a son.

Wayne Anderson's work has been used in advertising, magazines and for posters and greetings cards. He has made two animated films – one, featuring his drawings, was shown on British television – and has originated and illustrated two children's books, *Ratsmagic,* for which he won the American Society of Illustrators' gold medal, and *The Magic Circus*.